DEATH BEYOND THE WILLOWS

DEATH BEYOND THE WILLOWS

How a Wedding Day Turned Tragic in America's Heartland

by Greg Peck

The Guest Cottage
Woodruff, Wisconsin

In memory of Louis J. Klecker, Jr.
1930-2003

Acknowledgements

Thanks go, first and foremost, to my wife, Cheryl. Without her love, support and patience, I never would have started this project. Thanks also must go to my four key sounding boards—John Halverson and his wife, Liz Gall, and former co-worker Roger Miller, all of Janesville, and my high school journalism teacher, Jim Winters of rural Cottage Grove. Their guidance and encouragement will never be forgotten.

Others likewise have offered much support along the way, including two other co-workers, columnist Anna Marie Lux and reporter Carla McCann of *The Janesville Gazette*.

Also earning thanks is author Jerry Apps for helping lead me to Nancy Ravanelli and The Guest Cottage in Woodruff. I'm deeply thankful to Apps and Ben Logan for reviewing my manuscript and offering the thoughtful words that you'll find on the back cover. Logan's book, *The Land Remembers*, was an inspiration for the journey that led to this book.

Finally, I would be remiss in not thanking my parents for the countless questions they answered, and to other relatives and the dozens of people who opened their lives, minds and hearts to share their stories.

Published by
The Guest Cottage
Woodruff, Wisconsin

Designed by Patricia Bickner Linder

Greg Peck is editorial page editor of *The Janesville Gazette* in Janesville, Wis. He graduated from Marshall High School in 1975. A 1979 graduate of the University of Wisconsin-Oshkosh, he has worked and written for newspapers the past 27 years. He has won awards for sports, column, news and editorial writing.

Contents

Prologue

Joe Lindsay was a senior when I was a freshman at Marshall High School in Dane County, Wisconsin. Joe grew up in Deansville, a hamlet a couple of miles west of Marshall. Deansville was nothing more than a crossroads, with a feed mill and a few other businesses that had sprung up decades earlier around a railway stop. Joe loved to talk. "Keep them jaws a moving," it says under his photo in Marshall High's 1972 yearbook. He was a good friend of another senior, Randy Hellenbrand. Randy had dated my sister, Karen, when I was young and curious enough to sneak through one of our basement's three rec room doors to check out the amorous goings-on.

Joe and Randy ran on Marshall High's cross-country team. I did, too, and because the team was small and new, I ran varsity with a couple of other freshmen. It was a close-knit team that year, and we'd stop at the tiny Marshall Diner after practice and plop down on stools at the counter to enjoy luscious chocolate malts.

Randy and Joe were the type who couldn't resist having a good time, even if it meant playing practical jokes on each other. I'll never forget one in particular. We had practiced, showered, and were getting dressed in the boys locker room. But Joe couldn't find his jeans. I can still hear Joe with that nasally whine: "Hellenbraaaaand, where's my pants?" Randy had strung them up the flagpole, where they were blowing in the breeze.

Joe and Randy were out one night a couple of years later, apparently celebrating a birthday. Randy was driving, and though he was familiar with the roads, he somehow lost control on a curve just north of Deansville. The car rolled on its side. Joe flew out, struck his head, and died. The coroner estimated the time of death at 2:18 a.m., September 25, 1974. Joe Lindsay had turned 20 just two hours earlier. Sometimes, bad things happen to good people.

Newspaper columnist Harry F. Rosenthal once wrote that "every time an old man dies, a library burns down." As the new millennium approached, I was discovering how true those words were, not only about old men, but about old women, too.

This book focuses on the Pirkl family of Marshall. I began my research in late 1997 when I met Joann Ramseier of Janesville. It was less than two months after she had joined a gathering of older people at St. Mary's Catholic Church in Marshall to reflect, to remember, and to reminisce about an incident long ago. It was an event that would leave sorrow and heartache; one that, many decades later, would change my life and send me on a trail of research, study, and discovery.

A year into my effort, I was telling good friend and co-worker John Halverson about some of my findings. He commented that my project had become a quixotic journey. Webster's Dictionary defines quixotic, an adjective, as something "extravagantly chivalrous or romantically idealistic; visionary." He was right. I interviewed dozens of older people in those first 18 months. I talked to some individuals three, four, even five times. They allowed me into their lives, openly, honestly, willingly. They wove fascinating tales about growing up in Marshall. It was indeed a quixotic journey.

One day, in March 1999, I had called Joann Ramseier to ask a few more questions. Her comments made me step back. She expressed concern about where the research was going; about how deeply it would probe into the personal lives of people. I assured her I would omit all details she would not want published.

She didn't give specifics, but she re-emphasized her concern, nonetheless. That night, I slept little. What was I doing? Where would this venture lead? It seemed to be unleashing many sealed-up memories. Additionally, almost every time I interviewed someone, I found that the story being shared intersected with my own life; the history of the Pecks. It became obvious that Peck family details would be woven into this account, too.

A few days passed before I decided I could not turn back. The stories I had been chronicling were too powerful and compelling to abandon.

Every family has its scabs and closet skeletons. Alcohol abuse is one such scab among some of the Pirkls and their descendants. It also was part of my Grandpa Klecker's life, as it is a part of the saga of many families in small towns in the Midwest. Perhaps descendants of the Pirkls would prefer not to read the details of human frailty within the family. But to leave them out would be to strip this story of facts that say much about Marshall, about growing up there, and about a painful incident that happened there many years ago.

I do not wish to offend anyone. As a journalist, I desire to tell a story as fully and accurately as it has been told to me. My research verifies the fact that—sometimes bad things happen to good people.

I

Into the Fog

The wedding party, September 27, 1927, from left: flower girl Dorothy Walker, groom Johnny Pirkl, bride Hazel Ferguson, maid of honor Catherine Conrad and best man Cyril Langer.

A Gay and Romantic Ceremony

"It was like a dream wedding."

You can walk down Main Street in the little village of Marshall, Wisconsin, and never find a shred of evidence of the tragedy that took place in 1927.

It was a blow so profound, so devastating, so heart-breaking, that family, friends, and neighbors who lived through it gathered again 70 years later, in 1997, to reflect, remember, and mourn once again. Some of the mourners weren't even born in 1927. That says much about the type of community Marshall is—a once-quiet farming village in America's Dairyland, now a growing suburb of commuters.

Marshall remains a dot on the map of the upper Midwest, in America's Heartland. It is in Dane County, home of the state capital, Madison. The village is about 20 minutes east, slightly north, of the Badger State's governmental center. Marshall, population 3,432, is where this story begins, and ends.

Find the Roman Catholic Church, St. Mary of the Nativity. It's on Beebe Street, in the heart of the modest downtown. The simple modified Roman design features a bell tower stretching skyward. The building of reddish-brown brick was constructed in 1921 and remains the tallest in Marshall. In a way, this story begins and ends here, too.

Now drive around to St. Mary's back parking lot, and you'll notice a street leading out of town. It takes you past the high school and Holy Trinity Church, both built in recent years. You're now on County T, passing modest farmland that once supported small dairy herds. About two miles out of town, you'll see a clutch of white farm buildings and three silos on a little knoll. The place is known locally as the Darrell Langer farm. Hang a left directly across from the farm on—appropriately enough— Langer Road.

The road soon turns right; then it makes a hard left as it again heads south. You're passing more land where farmers once raised hay, corn, and oats for dairy cattle, hogs, and chickens. Soon, you're climbing a hill. Off to your right, close to the road, you'll see a white, two-story home. A mix of older deciduous trees stands near a pond, and younger pines grow between the road and the house. Cyril Langer, cousin to Darrell and the oldest of Edward and Theresa Langer's five children, was born here in 1903.

As you pass this farm, gaze beyond it. Behind a large stand of pines, you should spot the rooftops of another spread of buildings, the former Pirkl dairy farm.

The Pirkl buildings sit over a little rise that nearly obscures them from County T. But from this vantage point on Langer Road, you'll realize they're really sitting on a plain below another huge ridge. The steep, wooded crest you see in the distance to the west was part of the Pirkl farm. Langer Road follows the eastern ridge. The last place, at the end of Langer Road, is the Johnson farm, which spills down the slope toward the Pirkl property. Glaciers left these moraines thousands of years before the Pirkls, Langers, and Johnsons started calling the region home. From that farm of Cyril Langer's early childhood, it wasn't a far walk to the neighboring farm, where young Cyril got to know Johnny Pirkl.

Johnny and Cyril both entered adulthood during the 1920s, which was known as "The Roaring Twenties" and "The Jazz Age." During this decade, religious leaders fearfully pointed to suggestive dancing, necking, and rising hemlines as signs of moral decay. The 1920s also gave rise to racism behind the "Red Scare" and the growth of the Ku Klux Klan. Prohibition led to bootleggers, speakeasies, and turf wars between gangs. It was a decade of great feats, too, as baseball slugger Babe Ruth, heavy-

Hazel Ferguson and Johnny Pirkl posed in separate portraits on their wedding day. Below, the house that Hazel and Johnny were to move into upon their return from the honeymoon.

weight boxer Gene Tunney, and pioneer pilot Charles Lindbergh Jr. became household names.

Across the United States, the decade dawned as an era of great prosperity, despite the fact that President Woodrow Wilson, in the autumn of 1919, had suffered a stroke from which he would never recover. Warren G. Harding succeeded Wilson in 1920, but the likeable Republican from Ohio left a legacy of corruption before suffering a stroke and dying in August 1923. His vice president, Calvin Coolidge, took the reins. While urban businessmen were prospering, many farmers were struggling. By 1924, many Midwestern farmers—families like the Pirkls and Langers—sought farm relief, and scores turned to the Progressive Party and its nominee, Wisconsin Sen. Robert M. La Follette. Still, the nation elected to "Stay Cool with Coolidge."

The country's overall economic prosperity wouldn't last for long. But any sign of approaching calamity didn't deter Johnny Pirkl, farmer's son from Marshall, from planning a life, a future, with Hazel Ferguson, farmer's daughter from nearby Cottage Grove. In 1927, Coolidge announced to the nation that he would not seek re-election. And that same year, Johnny Pirkl and Hazel Ferguson announced to friends and family around Dane County their plans to marry.

Johnny Pirkl was the youngest of six siblings—three sisters and three brothers. But instead of choosing a brother, 26-year-old Johnny asked his friend Cyril Langer to be his best man and lone wedding attendant. And 22-year-old Hazel, with no close relatives similar in age, chose friend Catherine Conrad, also 22, of Sun Prairie as her maid of honor. Johnny and Hazel occasionally would climb into Johnny's new car, a 1927 Chevrolet, to make the trip to the Conrad home in downtown Sun Prairie, where Hazel and Catherine—Kay, they called her—would discuss the wedding plans.

While Hazel dreamed of the perfect ceremony, Johnny was focused on the days, months, and years beyond their vows. They would be a farm family, but it was time for Johnny to branch out on his own, to move off the home place, which was occupied by Johnny's brother Frank and Frank's new bride, Helen. In 1926, family patriarch Joseph Pirkl and his wife, Barbara, had moved off the homestead, leaving the hard sunup-to-sun-down labor to their two youngest sons. In November of that year, Joseph and Barbara's new home on the southwest edge of Marshall was complete. The two-story house featured a sprawling porch stretching across the entire front.

Johnny and Hazel had the good fortune of finding a farm for sale nearby. It was the Wakeman spread, owned by Fred and Effie Wakeman, on Highway TT, around the corner and northwest of the Pirkl homestead. It stood near the farm where Johnny's sister Alta and her husband, Ed Walker, worked the land. It's unknown whether Johnny's father helped him with the down payment on the Wakeman place. What is known is that Johnny signed his name to a land contract dated September 7, 1927. He put $1,000 down, and the balance—$7,307.50—was due November 1, 1927, to be paid with a five-year mortgage at four percent interest with payments of $100.

Johnny possibly could have collected a few spare tools and farm implements from the Pirkl homestead, but certainly not enough to supply his new farm. A week after buying the Wakeman place, he attended a George Fiebiger agent sale. Lydia Zimprich, the sale's secretary and treasurer, compiled a list of Johnny's purchases:

A wheelbarrow , $3.50
Ten grain sacks @ $.15 ea., $1.50
Twelve grain sacks @ $.125 ea., $1.50
A scythe , $0.25
A scraper and shovel, $1.00
Three clevises, $0.15
Oil cans and oil, $0.50
A three-horse seeder, $65.00
A mower, $45.00
A three-section drag, $25.00
A horse, $60.00

His total, $203.40, was a handsome sum in those days.

Johnny and Hazel had a bridal shower at the old Medina Town Hall, across the street from St. Mary's Catholic Church. Ironically, the building later was moved and used for storage on the Darrell Langer farm. "They had a dance, and Hazel opened presents and announced each one," longtime Marshall resident Jim Langer recalled of the shower.

The town hall had a little room on each side of the entry. One was for coats, the other for serving food. At dances, someone would sell tickets to the couples from a small ticket window on the right. People would walk in and step onto a big dance floor. A stage stood on the east end. The furnace was below the stage. "You could feel the floor sag when you were to step into that old town hall," recalled Jim, cousin to both Cyril and Darrell Langer.

Jim found a bit of irony in having the town hall across from the Catholic church. "They always said that there were more souls made than saved around there. Young guys would take their girls over there to the town hall and make out. It was open."

Autumn colors were nowhere near full bloom in southern Wisconsin on September 27, 1927. Not that it would have mattered. The morning dawned as another in a series of dull, dreary, and foggy days in Dane County. It was a Tuesday, and the wedding was set for 9 a.m., a day and time that seem odd to us in an era when most weddings occur on Saturday afternoons. But the timing was not uncommon back then.

All of Johnny's siblings had already wed, and some of them had bigger wedding parties. Besides Johnny's niece, five-year-old Dorothy Walker, daughter of Alta and Ed Walker, serving as flower girl, Johnny and Hazel opted for just one attendant each; again, not an uncommon practice back then. The focus of a Catholic service in those days was on the bride and groom, not on a big production featuring the other people in the wedding party.

Over at Joe Pirkl's new home in Marshall, his soon-to-be daughter-in-law, Hazel Ferguson, pulled on her white leggings. She slipped into her knee-length wedding dress. Then she slid into her white high heels and secured the single strap on each. She placed the veil on her head, the flowing, see-through georgette nearly touching the floor. With her white-gloved hands, she picked up her attractive bouquet of pink roses, strips of ribbons cascading off it. She was ready to meet her groom.

At the Pirkl farm, Johnny washed in the cramped tub, likely after another morning of barn chores, and he combed back his dark hair. He put on his shirt and tie, and his dark, double-breasted suit coat. He pinned a boutonniere into the pocket on his left side and slipped into his shiny black dress shoes, spit-polished. Then he hopped into his dark gray Chevy and drove into Marshall. He was ready to meet his bride.

It was a beautiful wedding, the guests evenly distributed on each side of the aisle. Johnny and Hazel had a lot of friends, but it was still a small wedding. "I remember walking down the aisle," the flower girl recalled 70-some years later. "Mom had a vivid blue outfit on; I would focus my eyes on her to ease my fears."

Two more of Johnny's nieces, Catherine Benesch and Helen Springer, were 11 and eight, respectively. Helen would never forget the gay and romantic ceremony. "It was a beautiful wedding. Catherine and I were older, so we took care of my little sister and the other little kids during the wedding. She had big roses, a beautiful bouquet," Helen said of Hazel. "It was like a dream wedding. She was just a vision. Johnny was so handsome with his wavy, black hair. He looked like Robert Taylor, the actor, only he was probably better looking than Taylor."

"Johnny was such a handsome man," agreed Sue (Catherine) Woerpel, who was about 13 at the time and whose brother, Bill Hamshire, was another of Johnny's good friends. "I always thought he'd be a good man. That's what you think when you're just a kid."

Father Christian M. Nellen said the Mass in Latin and faced the altar during Latin prayers. Likewise, the altar boy, 13-year-old Nathan Baker, answered in Latin. Instead of a friend or relative doing the readings, Father Nellen read from the Bible in English. Nellen turned to face Johnny and Hazel as they likely pledged to love, honor, and obey, in sickness and in health, in good times and in bad, for richer or poorer, until death do we part.

Afterward, Johnny and Hazel stepped into a side room at the church to sign their marriage license, a document issued three days earlier. It named Catherine Conrad and Cyril Langer as attendants, Christian Nellen as priest. It listed Johnny's occupation as "farmer" and Hazel's as "at home."

That certificate had remained among family heirlooms more than 70 years when descendants noticed that someone had gone to great pains to ink out a couple of words next to where Johnny and Hazel had signed their names. The words were "bride" and "groom." After their vows, Johnny and Hazel had signed on the wrong lines.

It wouldn't be the last mistake they'd make that day.

As the newlyweds left the church, guests threw rice, and the small wedding party departed for Sun Prairie to pose for portraits. In one, Johnny sat alone on a bench, a hand on a knee, the other on a short podium, looking relaxed, confident, proud, and happy. Hazel, too, posed alone in one, standing, a slight smile visible, her veil nearly touching the floor. In another, Johnny sat to the right of his brightly smiling bride.

Yet another photo included the entire wedding party: little Dorothy standing on the left side, holding her ring pillow; Johnny grinning while standing behind his sitting bride; Catherine Conrad, seated next to Hazel, clothed in a wavy pink taffeta dress coming just below the knee—stylish for the day but cut a bit too high for the tastes of older women—white leggings and shoes, feet crossed, her hat's wide brim pointing up on her left, down on her right; Cyril Langer standing on the right side, dressed in a single-breasted suit coat a bit lighter in color than Johnny's, a boutonniere pinned to his left lapel. Their faces tell perhaps what they're thinking: Johnny's smile indicative of true happiness; Hazel's expression a bit anxious, perhaps wishing it was all over; Catherine looking confident, perhaps prissy; Cyril maybe thinking "let's get this over with"; little Dorothy standing there only because Mommy said she had to.

At about 1 p.m., the Pirkl family and close friends, about 25 in all, gathered for a big dinner at the home of Johnny's parents in Marshall. It was only a couple of blocks from the church. As many as possible crowded around Barbara Pirkl's huge oak table, the one she brought to town from the farm. The table had eight-foot wide inserts, a middle leg at each end of the split lending support. The mammoth table, which seated 24, stretched from the dining room into the living room.

Flowers from the ceremony decorated the home, their overpowering fragrance enough to make sickly little Catherine Benesch feel ill. As was customary at such family gatherings, there was singing and much gaiety. Johnny's sister Edie Benesch "tickled the ivories," while his mother cranked up her phonograph with the big speaker. Maid of honor Catherine Conrad played songs on her 12-string ukulele. For being so good and doing everything expected of her, little Dorothy received a doll draped in a pink dress from her new Aunt Hazel.

"They were throwing rice and having a good time," said Eugene Schenck, who was 12 at the time and always walked past the house on his way to and from school. "I saw Johnny's mother sweeping up rice off the floor. I saw the new Chevy parked out front."

All too soon, at about 4 p.m., it was time for Johnny and Hazel to depart for their wedding trip to Pine City, Minnesota, where they planned to visit Johnny's other brother, Ed, and his family. Hazel slipped out of her wedding dress and changed into traveling clothes. She pinned her corsage to her coat. Johnny still wore his rosebud boutonniere.

Hazel climbed into Johnny's Chevy and looped the strap of a silver mesh bag containing a prayer book—a wedding present—around a dashboard knob. Johnny and Hazel smiled and waved as they drove off into the fog that still shrouded the landscape, leaving the family with an uneasy feeling. Tied to the back of Johnny's gray auto were the traditional items—a "Just Married" sign, an old shoe, and tins dangling and making a ruckus as the couple drove off in the fading daylight. Some 70 years later, Johnny and Hazel's flower girl recalled waving while her grandmother expressed concern and cried, tears rolling down her big cheeks.

"I can always remember them driving away—that I do remember quite vividly," Dorothy said. "It wasn't quite dark yet. I can remember my Grandma saying to Johnny, 'You shouldn't go tonight, Johnny. It's too foggy.'" But the happy couple apparently had plans to spend the night in Baraboo and departed despite Barbara's misgivings.

Dorothy will never forget what happened the next day at the Walker home. "Mom saw Sorenson's hearse go by our house, heading west, and she said, 'Something's happened to Johnny, I just know it.' She cried and cried. But Dad said, 'You don't even know what it's about.' But she had a premonition."

The Walkers got a phone call after the hearse went by. Dorothy recalled, "There was a lot of crying."

Joseph Pirkl (r.) with two of his sons, Frank (l.) and Johnny, and his prized horses at the farm in Marshall, c. 1911. Below, Joseph and Barbara Pirkl's family, c. 1918. Back row: Frank, Edith, Martha, Edward; Front row: Alta, Joseph, Barbara and Johnny.

The Pirkls

"It was always a happy time when Johnny paid a visit."

Joseph and Frances Pirkl were Bohemians who very likely fled German persecution in Europe. An obituary for the former Frances Stransky lists her birth year as 1821 and says she arrived in America in 1854. Joseph and Frances caught a ship sailing across the Atlantic and arrived on the East Coast. Eventually, they traveled west to Wisconsin, a state then six years old, and settled in Milford Township in Jefferson County.

Milford, today, is a river burg at the crossroads of County A and County Q, north of Interstate 94, which runs between Madison and the state's largest city, Milwaukee. Milford, a few miles northeast of the small city of Lake Mills, is little more than a handful of houses and a bar. A used car dealer and Vandre's Riverside Inn closed in recent years. Each spring, anglers fish along the banks of the Crawfish River, pulling chunky walleyes from the turbulent water during the spawning run. Other fishermen stand in the shallows downstream from the bridge, casting their hopes into the murky waters.

This rural township is where Joseph and Frances Pirkl raised two sons on a farmstead: John was born in 1856, and Joseph Jr. in 1860. But Frances was widowed at a young age. John was four, and Joseph was only a one-year-old when their father died at age 38. His will, listing separate parcels of 40 and 20 acres in the township, was recorded in 1867, leading some descendants to believe that was the year he died. In fact, some of Joseph Jr.'s grandchildren had heard that their grandpa was seven years old when Joseph Sr. died. However, Watertown's St. Henry Catholic Church recorded the date of death as July 10, 1861; another researcher claimed church records put it on November 10 of that year. Assuming that he died in 1861, it's unknown why it took so long to record the will, which appointed John Duschack as guardian of the minor children.

The Stransky family had settled in the village of Marshall, which is about 11 miles northwest of Milford. Relatives on the Stransky side helped the widow Frances Pirkl and her two sons relocate to a little house on County T. In 1867, she bought what would be known as the Pirkl farm, which had passed through two sets of hands after being acquired from the state in 1849. Whether the widow Pirkl's little home was actually on that farmland from the beginning is uncertain; it is thought that the farmhouse in which her son Joseph would eventually raise his family once stood closer to present-day County T. One can only imagine the enormous task of moving a home—likely pulled atop rolling logs by stout workhorses or oxen—in those days.

Frances Pirkl deeded the farm to Joseph, then 21, in 1881. The wording of a "bond for maintenance" says much about the era:

Joseph " . . . do hereby agree to support and take care of Frances Perkle (sic) . . . during the term of her natural life and for that purpose do agree to furnish her with board, clothing, bed, bedding, house, room, fire wood and have her washing done for her and to do each and everything that may be necessary to do to make her comfortable as long as the said Frances Perkle shall live . . . "

But why deed the farm to Joseph and not to her older son, John? The answer is the first in a series of sad chapters in the Pirkl family's history. It seems that John ran away from home at age 21 and was never heard from again. No one knew why he left, or where he went. "Grandpa searched and searched, hired detectives, hired a fortune teller," Marian Zimbric said of her Grandpa, Joseph Pirkl, Jr. "He never got a clue about him."

In 1887, at age 26, Joseph Jr. married the former Barbara Hady at St. Henry's in Watertown, one of the key cities in the migration west from Milwaukee. Like her in-laws, Barbara Hady came to the United States from Bohemia. Barbara, born in 1865, was only three years old when she arrived in this country with her parents, Frank Hady and the former Katherine Novotny. The family apparently buried Barbara's little sister at sea. Barbara had an older sister, Mary, born in 1853. The girls had three brothers: John, Michael, and Thomas.

Frank and Katherine Hady, like so many immigrants, rode the train from Milwaukee to Watertown, where they settled, died, and were buried. Meanwhile, their three boys migrated west to Oakes, North Dakota. But all eventually drifted back to Minnesota, farmed land near Pine City, and died there.

Joseph and Barbara Pirkl were devout Catholics whose first child, Ed, was born on Valentine's Day in 1888. More than two years later, in 1890, Edith arrived. Then came siblings Martha, Frank, and Alta. On July 6, 1901, Johnny was born.

Six was not an unusual number of kids for a farm family in Marshall. Henry and Zara Peck raised a family of six across County T from the Pirkls. Other local families had 10 or more children. However, Barbara Pirkl actually bore seven children in that farmhouse. Elleonora was born in 1914, when her mother was 48 and her father nearly 54. But her young life led to some of the first pangs of heartache for the Pirkl family. Elleonora died of pneumonia that same year. It's likely that Johnny, Elleonora's youngest sibling at just age 13, felt great sorrow over the loss of his baby sister. Johnny enjoyed people and loved kids. It seems logical that he, too, dreamed of raising a large family.

Ed was the first of the Pirkl siblings to wed. In 1911, Ed was 23 when he married Josephine Schuster, 22, in Sun Prairie. Josie was the daughter of Anton Schuster and the former Theresa Stangler. The Schuster family lived on a hilltop west of Marshall on what today is Highway 19.

Six other adults, a flower girl, and a ring-bearer made up the couple's unusually large wedding party. A photograph shows the group, all with stoical faces, the common expression in photos back then. The round-faced Josie and the somewhat ruddy-faced Ed stood on one end. Ed's oldest sisters, Edith—Edie, they called her—and Martha joined him in the wedding party, as did his oldest brother, Frank, then a handsome but big-eared boy of 15. Loren Hebl carried the rings; at age 10, Johnny Pirkl perhaps was considered too old for the job.

The newlyweds planned to join Ed's uncles from the Hady family in farming Minnesota's Pine City area. That decision would bring tragic consequences.

Less than 15 months after Ed's wedding, Joseph Pirkl gave away his first daughter. The slender Edie wed Edward Benesch in 1913 in Sun Prairie. Serving as witnesses for Edie and Edward were Martha Pirkl and Edward Walker, the latter a friend of the groom who eventually would marry a Pirkl girl himself.

Edward Benesch and his new bride joined his parents on the Benesch farmstead on Highway 73 on Marshall's north end.

Martha was the next Pirkl to marry, in 1918. She wed Leonard Springer at St. Mary's, Father Nellen presiding. The wedding took place in a wooden chapel that previously served a Baptist congregation; the little structure was razed and gave way to St. Mary's new brick church by the time Johnny wed. Springer, 24 on his wedding day, was a talented musician and farmer who lived with his parents, Charles Springer and the former Agnes Packel, on a hilltop spread on rolling Canal Road between Marshall and Waterloo. The newlyweds would start farming on the same road, closer to Waterloo; just one farmstead separated father's farm from his son's.

Frank Pirkl, by then nearly 22, stood up with the tall Leonard and Leonard's even-taller brother, Walter, whose curly red hair was piled oddly atop his head. Joining Martha in the wedding party was her sister Alta. A wedding photo shows the Pirkl girls, who could nearly pass for twins, both staring off. The groom looks confident, while the bride shows no happiness in her bland expression.

Perhaps the bride was unhappy about the bouquets she and her attendants were holding. The flowers were severely wilted by the time the group arrived at the photo studio. Leonard's mother wouldn't allow the couple to leave the wedding party early to get photos taken.

It's likely that Barbara, Joseph, and their family of six posed for a portrait at this time. No one knows the date for sure, but in the portrait, Frank looks identical to the way he does in the Springer wedding photo. And the

Edward Walker and Alta Pirkl on their wedding day, April 13, 1920. From left: Catherine Benesch, Alta Pirkl, Edward Walker, Edward's sister Hattie Drunasky, Johnny Pirkl and Lucille Benesch, future wife of Jim Langer. Below, left: Frank Pirkl and Helen Holzman on their wedding day, November 24, 1925. Below, right: Pirkl sisters Martha and Alta (in front) dressed in their finest, c. 1913.

handsome Johnny, seated with suit, bow tie, and high-top lace shoes, looks to be a boy about ready to turn 17. Besides, it would take a significant event such as a wedding to get Ed to leave Minnesota for a visit—in those days likely a whole day's travel by train.

In the portrait, Joseph looks suave, debonair, stately, self-confident, and happy with life. His wife, Barbara, also bears the look of contentment, as though she knows she's done a good job raising her family. Johnny looks a tad serious, young enough to not know what's going on, just happy to be in the picture.

Alta would be the next to wed, repeating vows with the aforementioned Edward Walker in the spring of 1920 at St. Mary's; C.M. Nellen again presiding. Johnny, though only 18, stood up as best man with Hattie Drunasky, Edward's sister.

The wedding photo shows the round-faced Alta and the attractive Hattie seated—Alta wearing an elaborate headpiece in contrast to Hattie's light-colored, wide-brimmed hat. Alta's bouquet also was fancy, ribbons adorning it. Behind Alta stood the striking groom, with a double-breasted suit, white shirt, and tie. Beside him stood Johnny, who wore a similar shirt and tie. But Johnny's dark, single-breasted suit had a belt wrapping his mid-section. While the bride and, perhaps, even the groom appear a bit tense, Johnny looks relaxed and easy-going. Flanking the four were Alta's petite and uncomfortable-looking niece, Catherine Benesch, with light hair and hands together; and the taller, dark-haired, smug-faced Lucille Benesch. The little cousins carried matching flower baskets.

Johnny was close to Alta, so it's no wonder he stood up in her wedding. He was also close to his brother Frank. The two young men were still working the Pirkl farm together when Frank married Helen Holzman in November 1925 at St. Joseph Catholic Church in East Bristol, Helen's hometown. A wedding photo shows the somewhat stocky Helen standing next to her taller and attractive husband. Both appear fashionable, dressed to the hilt, the bride in a straight-hanging dress.

Helen was a farmer's daughter; her parents had arrived from Germany and had another daughter and a son, neither of whom ever married. Like many Germans, Helen was a good cook, and Johnny enjoyed many fine meals after hard days of toil in the fields with Frank.

By the time true love blossomed for Johnny, he had a bunch of nieces and nephews. Edie and Edward Benesch had three children—Catherine, 11, Leo, nine, and Jim, not yet two years old. Martha and Leonard Springer had two daughters, Helen, eight, and Margie, a month younger than her cousin Jim. Alta and Edward Walker had two children, Dorothy, five, and Robert, three years old.

Uncle Johnny was closest to Dorothy and Robert, likely because of proximity; the Walkers were farming on County T, just beyond Pyburn School where County T and TT split; the place was about a mile from the Pirkl farm.

Johnny had seven nieces and nephews in the Marshall area. But he had another six in Pine City. Ed and Josie Pirkl's youngest child, Dorothy Emily, was born in February 1927. No doubt, Johnny was excited about the prospects of visiting Ed and getting acquainted with his baby niece and her siblings in Minnesota.

It was always a happy time when her Uncle Johnny paid a visit to the Walker farm, Dorothy remembered of the days when she was just five years old. She recalled Johnny as a happy, kind man. Because he was so close to her mother, he stopped in every week or so. He'd always play with Dorothy and her younger brother Bob.

During one such visit, on a sunny day in 1927, Johnny and others snapped several photos with Johnny's camera, a box-type device in which the user had to look down into the viewfinder. The photos are poignant, playful, and revealing. Several snapshots show a young woman. Her name was Hazel Ferguson.

In their new home at 227 Porter Street, Barbara and Joseph Pirkl had their bedroom on the first floor, and the second story opened to two more bedrooms. Later on, the Pirkls boarded female teachers in the upstairs bedrooms. But in the fall of 1927, someone else moved in temporarily. It was their future daughter-in-law, Hazel Ferguson.

A young Hazel Ferguson strikes an attractive portrait pose.

An Only Child

"Catholics never encouraged mixed marriages . . . "

Like Johnny Pirkl, Hazel Mary Ferguson was raised on a farm. But unlike Johnny, she had no brothers or sisters. Hazel was born June 16, 1905, to John Ferguson and the former Ida Akin. A lack of descendants in Hazel's family makes details of her life sketchy.

Hazel's paternal grandparents, Louise and Henry Ferguson, died in 1914 and 1916, respectively. They're buried, along with Henry's parents, Daniel and Gertrude Ferguson, in Pierceville Cemetery, a plot of mostly aging markers on a little knoll between Marshall and Cottage Grove.

When Hazel Ferguson was in her teens, she, her parents, and her father's brother, Carl, occupied a sprawling farmhouse that still stands on County TT, outside Cottage Grove on the way to Marshall.

The large size of Johnny's family likely, in part, attracted Hazel to him. The fun-loving spirit of Johnny and others in his family made for wonderful times. Parents and kids worked side by side in the barn, the fields, and the garden. Christian holidays were times of big get-togethers, of jovial celebration, and of lavish meals. The hustle and bustle of a bigger family, with lots of activity, likely intrigued Hazel.

As a child, Hazel often walked a mile or more, through all kinds of weather, to Gaston School, which was halfway between the Ferguson farm and Cottage Grove. Adjacent to the schoolhouse sat the Bulman farm, where Hazel's distant cousins, Phoebe and Neil, resided.

The school was built in 1910 to replace a stone structure. It stood on what was known as Gaston Corners, named for Albert Gaston, a Massachusetts man whose family owned land in that part of Cottage Grove Township. The school's front entrance was in the southeast corner, half a dozen steps up. Above the doorway rose a bell tower. Schoolchildren often dared to shimmy up the bell tower to a trap door leading to the attic, where they'd carve their initials in the rafters.

The square, one-room school was painted white, and it had no basement. A wood stove heated it. Kids piled coats in one of two cloakrooms. The schoolyard was large, perfect for burning off energy at recess. An outhouse stood in the back corner. In summer, children could play on a makeshift ball diamond. In winter, the students would sled from the top of a hill on the Bulman farm down into the schoolyard.

Gaston School stands today, minus its bell tower, but with a basement. A single man restored the school, turning it into his living quarters. Beyond the former Bulman farm runs Interstate 94, intersecting the land between the school and the former Ferguson farm.

Cottage Grove grew up around a railway stop eight miles east of Madison. Rolling lands of prairie, oaks, and meadows surround the village, which was named after a burr oak grove where a public house served as the community's first post office. This information was compiled in 1976 by the Cottage Grove Historical Committee.

Farming is an integral part of the community's history. It's fitting, then, that Cottage Grove was home to Wisconsin's 12th governor, Col. William Taylor, who championed farm causes and became known as the "Granger" governor. For more than 100 years, the land has yielded top-notch hay and provided quality pastures for farmers. Even early on, fine farmhouses and barns reflected thrift and social independence.

When Hazel's Uncle Carl bought the Ferguson place from Wince Drunzskey in 1909, it had gone through several ownership changes. But

Carl and John would own it more than three decades before selling the 200-acre spread to Ludwig Stohl and his wife in 1941. Stohl owned the Wisconsin Porcelain Company in Sun Prairie, a business started by his father, August, who learned the trade in Germany.

The dairy barn, now double in size, sits near the foot of a steep hillside not far from the house and close to the back property line. The Ferguson brothers also had a corncrib and other outbuildings typical of a dairy operation of the day.

Today, the Ferguson farmhouse, painted a light yellow, stands within earshot of Interstate 94, where thousands of commuters, truckers, and vacationers pass daily. Most of the original farmland across County TT butted up to the present-day freeway. When Hazel was growing up, it was a quiet, serene place. Koshkonong Creek bubbled and gurgled as it meandered across the countryside, dissecting it in odd ways. Water flowed into a pond on one spot, providing an idyllic winter place for Hazel and her Bulman cousins, little Phoebe and her older brother, Neil, to ice skate.

The Ferguson farmhouse sits close to the road and has a porch across the front and another one off the kitchen. During Hazel's childhood days, it certainly didn't look like the home of a family struggling to survive on what must have been a modest dairy farm income. A passerby might say, judging from the attractive home, that there was little doubt who ruled in the Ferguson farmhouse. The home had spacious rooms, hardwood floors, and nine-foot ceilings. And it was well-maintained. The Fergusons weren't spendthrifts; they took care of what they had.

The inviting kitchen was inside the main entryway, and a pantry was located nearby. When John Ferguson wasn't tending to his dairy cattle, he would sit in the kitchen in a comfortable chair and read his newspaper or gaze out the window.

An open stairway in the middle of the home led to four upstairs bedrooms. Another bedroom was downstairs in the southwest corner, and a living room—or sitting room—was in the southeast corner. Sliding wood doors divided the sitting room from the large parlor and dining room in the northeast corner. The dining room had a bay window facing north, and a door leading to the front porch featured a large oval window. A built-in china cabinet opened by way of glass doors from the dining room and by means of plain wood doors from the kitchen.

Fine furnishings and lamps and other things not seen in most farm-houses of that era filled the home. But despite all its amenities, the Ferguson home was like the Pirkl home in one key way: It had no indoor plumbing. Until the Stohls bought and remodeled it and dug a well, in the early 1940s, the home had kerosene lanterns instead of electric lighting, and an outhouse instead of running water and toilets.

By the year 2000, residential properties in Cottage Grove were hot options for commuters working in Madison. The census that year showed a growth rate that left village President David Conklin stunned. From 1990 to 2000, other Madison suburban communities had grown 20 percent, 30 percent, and even 50 percent, including Marshall's surge of 47 percent, from 2,329 to 3,432 people. But Cottage Grove had grown from 1,131 in 1990 to 4,059—a whopping 259 percent. Had Hazel Ferguson lived to see it, she likely would have been taken aback to see such growth in her hometown.

Likewise, she would have been shocked to see what was sprouting on the farmland her father and Uncle Carl once worked. In late 2001, travelers along Interstate 94 could see earth-moving equipment at work. Attorney Dennis Sieg bought the portion of the farm with the buildings in 1993. He and his wife live in the former Ferguson farmhouse. But B Farms, owned by the Blaska family of Sun Prairie/Marshall, bought the 170 or so acres across County TT. The family developed The Oaks Golf Course, which opened in 2003. A small subdivision for 14 homes is springing up adjacent to it.

Apparently, no photograph exists that shows the Ferguson farm the way it was when Hazel lived there. Nor does anyone have a photo of Hazel's parents. Johnny Pirkl must not have felt at liberty to bring his box camera to Hazel's home during their courtship.

However, one photo shows a striking image of Hazel, who looks young, perhaps no older than a teen, and sensual. Her dress features thin shoulder straps. Tiny white dots sprinkle the dark material, which fades into the photo's equally dark background. Hazel's hair is parted on the left, and she's looking toward the left; lips full. These days, someone might consider her fetching.

Another poignant photo shows an attractive Hazel, sometime in the days or weeks before her wedding, wearing a light-colored dress, dark

Joseph and Barbara Pirkl with their future daughter-in-law, Hazel Ferguson, outside their home in the village of Marshall.

shoes, and sleek white leggings. She's smiling and sitting on the knee of Joseph Pirkl, her future father-in-law. Joe is sitting in his beloved rocker, next to the front porch outside his home in Marshall. He's wearing a white shirt, dark slacks, shoes, and tie. His forehead is nearly as white as his hair, and the tan line on his face shows that he often wears a hat. Joe's wife, the stocky-looking Barbara, is also dressed in white and standing next to him. The photo is poignant because Hazel probably was living with Joe and Barbara at the time.

It's said that love conquers all. In this case, that must have been true. In the first place, Johnny Pirkl's plans to marry Hazel Ferguson drove a stake through the Ferguson family. It had nothing to do with the fact that Hazel was nearly four years younger than Johnny. Instead, the issue was religion. To marry Johnny, Hazel planned to change religions, to convert to Catholicism. The idea so upset the Fergusons that Hazel moved temporarily into the home of Joseph and Barbara Pirkl, and Hazel's father and mother vowed not to attend the wedding.

Then Johnny bought the Wakeman place, intending that he and his bride would call it home. For Hazel Ferguson, it was a commitment to a major change in lifestyle. The Ferguson farmhouse was large and roomy, and it featured many fine appointments. The Wakeman house was in stark contrast to the one in which Hazel grew up. This home had a small kitchen on the north side, which faced the barn and other outbuildings. In the kitchen stood a wood stove, the home's only source of heat. The ceilings were no higher than seven feet. Round log joists propped up floors that were slanted. The living room was to the southwest, where an L-shaped staircase led to two bedrooms on the second floor.

At age 22, on Monday, September 19, 1927, Hazel Ferguson was baptized into the Catholic faith at St. Mary's. Father Nellen performed the baptism, and Alta Walker, who would become Hazel's sister-in-law eight days later, was her sponsor.

Because Hazel had been baptized into a different church as a child, her conditional baptism in the Catholic faith came after conversion instruction that involved perhaps 15 or 20 one-on-one sessions with Father Nellen. Then, she professed that she believed in the Catholic faith and was baptized with holy water.

Also, at this time, Johnny and Hazel were attending instructional sessions on the fundamentals of faith and the sacrament of marriage.

Johnny and Hazel looked forward to a happy future, but they no doubt felt pangs in the pits of their stomachs and aches in their hearts over the opinions of Hazel's parents. Seventy-some years later, Monsignor Raymond Klaas, who led St. Mary's into the new millennium, put the rift into perspective.

"It wasn't uncommon, before the ecumenical movement, for a minister not to ever talk to a priest," he explained. "Now, you have prayer services together during holidays.

"First, we're human beings, we're Christians; even if we're not Christians, we're still human beings. Today, we still have ministers not having anything to do with priests. But that's a human invention; that's not the Lord's way. Christ came for everybody. Catholics never encouraged mixed marriages because marriages had enough problems; which faith to raise the children in would cause lots of emotional upheaval.

"Years ago, non-Catholics wouldn't step foot in a Catholic Church. That's all changed."

Farm Life

"The belt jumped off, and Johnny went after it.
He got his feet tangled up."

Danger always lurked on a farm in the 1920s. A fall from a haymow, a runaway horse, an angry bull—any number of potential hazards lay in wait for the careless farmer.

Mike Peck and his oldest brother, Bob, would often go to the neighboring Pirkl house at night to play euchre—a card game—with Johnny and his brother Frank. But not when Zara Peck was watching her sons. The Pecks were Methodists, and card games were strictly forbidden.

Mike recalled an incident when he and Johnny were operating a single-cylinder engine that ran a corn shredder, "Just a big thing you pulled around on wheels." Mike couldn't remember who was there besides Johnny and him. Anyway, the fellas started up the shredder, and Johnny went to engage the contraption by way of a wheel with a belt on it.

"The belt jumped off, and Johnny went after it," Mike recalled. "He got his feet tangled up. The belt was headed toward the engine and winding around the engine. He was just lucky he got untangled before it got to the engine. Otherwise, it would have been a catastrophe."

The middle one of the five Peck brothers recalled Johnny's fun-loving ways. Homer Peck, born in 1917, was nine when Johnny and Hazel wed. But one memory of Johnny was forever etched in his mind: a scene that involved Johnny and Frank Pirkl, and Homer and Bob Peck.

"Bob and I were at the Pirkl farm one snowy day," Homer said of the spring of 1927. "We had a snowball fight. Frank, Bob, and I were throwing at Johnny. We were by the cow barn; a cow tank was nearby. Johnny was laughing and hollering and having a helluva time. He was in the horse barn, with the half-door closed on the bottom, hollering at us to throw snowballs at him. As the snowballs arrived, he'd shut the top half of the door to shield himself from them."

Those scenes define the life of Johnny Pirkl—a hard-working man who was not so serious that he couldn't take time out for play. They are themes repeated again and again by his descendants, neighbors, and friends.

The Pirkl family's neighbors over the ridge to the west were William and Martha Pautsch. They raised five daughters and a son, Bob.

"Johnny was a really friendly person, always joking and stuff like that," said Bob, born in 1913. "I don't ever remember him getting mad or swearing. He was good-hearted. He liked fun, to tell stories, and joke around.

"The Pirkls were real good farmers. They didn't have corn full of weeds; they took care of it."

Neighbor-helping-neighbor was a way of farm life in the days of horses—the days before tractors pulled plows through rich soil and harvesting equipment through mature crops. "We worked together, exchanged help," Bob Pautsch said of his family and the Pirkls. "We'd thrash together, rig up a saw, and saw wood with Frank."

The Pirkl farmhouse had a big pot-belly wood-burning stove; no furnace warmed the place. "My dad had a saw, and we'd go to the Pirkls to saw wood. That was always a day's work to go saw wood for firewood with a 36-to-40-inch blade."

Neighbors even teamed up to prepare meat. "One of the Pirkls would come over and help butcher," Bob Pautsch said. "We'd cook up meat and can it—pork, ham, and bacon. We'd salt the pork down and make our own sausage."

Rachel Pautsch Kessler also remembered her neighbors to the east. In fact, Rachel took lessons on the mandolin from Johnny's sister Martha.

"He was a very likeable guy," Rachel said of Johnny. "They were good neighbors, a very fine family. My mother and dad were very fond of the Pirkl family, always respected each other. They were Catholic. We were Lutheran, so our church activities were different. But we were very friendly."

Frank Pirkl's youngest daughter, Joann, recalled her father's stories about life with Johnny. "Dad always talked about how they'd do silly stuff; sneak homemade wine and get a little silly on it; smoke rolled cigarettes; crazy kids' stuff."

The brothers also raced the farm horses, riding them bareback. "I think Johnny was a real character," Joann said. "Everybody liked him. He was fun-loving, honest, and thoughtful. They were fun-loving brothers who were really close. They worked hard together and played hard."

"Johnny Pirkl was very smiley, had a very great personality," recalled Jim Langer, former grade school principal in Marshall. "One of the things he always said—he didn't care if he had any money or not, but he had to have a lot of friends. Friendship was a great thing with him."

A Bend in the Road

"Johnny wasn't certain of his way out of town."

Johnny and Hazel Pirkl almost certainly discussed hopes and dreams as their gray Chevy coach knifed through the fog as they headed west toward Madison, then north on Highway 51 toward Portage. They likely reflected on family and friends who celebrated their wedding with them, and on those who didn't— on Hazel's disappointment at not seeing her parents show up at the ceremony to surprise her. Perhaps the couple discussed starting their own family.

Johnny possibly struggled to keep the car on the road in the fog. The car had no windshield defroster. A lone wiper blade—thinner, but no longer than a pencil—reached down from its mount atop the windshield to clean a small area of glass in front of his face, beyond the bulky wooden steering wheel. The roads were primitive—rough or unpaved, lacking center and edge stripes. Even on paved surfaces, potholes likely emerged from the shroud of fog.

It was after 6 p.m. when they made their way into Portage, glad to be there but determined to make their way to a hotel in Baraboo, perhaps the Wellington or the Warren. Whether they'd made reservations is uncertain because no records exist for either hotel; the Warren burned in the 1960s, and the Wellington was remodeled into office space. The bride and groom likely anticipated consummating their marriage at the hotel before rising the next morning and continuing their journey toward Pine City.

The Chevy was running low on gasoline, so Johnny looked for a service station. The couple arrived at the spot where Highway 16 came from the east and merged with Highway 51. They crossed a little bridge over the Portage Canal, a two-mile-long channel built in 1876 to enable boats to navigate between the Fox River and the Wisconsin River. Just past the bridge, Highway 16 veered off to the west. Johnny stayed on Highway 51, known then, as now, as DeWitt Street. A half block later, he came to Wright Motor Company. The Ford dealership's gas pump was at the curb. Johnny pulled up, and the newlyweds likely got out for a stretch. It was about 6:30 p.m. An attendant pumped ethyl gas into the glass bulb atop the pump and then let it drain down through the hose into the car's rear gas tank.

Darkness was falling, as was rain, further diminishing visibility in the fog, which was even thicker in Portage because the rivers added humidity to the air. Johnny wasn't certain of his way out of town. He asked the men at Wright's for directions. They urged him to reconsider continuing on, especially if he didn't know the way. But Johnny was unwavering in his plan. After all, Baraboo was about 17 miles farther, and they had traveled roughly 50 miles.

Johnny paid for the gas, thanked the men for their assistance, and bride and groom got back in the car. Johnny started the engine, pulled out, and, at the next downtown intersection, he turned left onto Cook Street, or Highway 33, which led toward Baraboo. The intersection was known as "bank corner," and through the fog, the couple probably noticed the bank that stood on the left, already closed for business for the day.

A block later, where Highway 16 again crossed their path, they must have noticed the Raulf Hotel, a beautiful five-story structure built on the northwest corner after the previous hotel was demolished a year earlier. Assuming the new hotel was already open for business, and because it was a Tuesday, there were likely vacancies. But Johnny didn't stop.

The bride and groom continued up Cook Street, the Chevy climbing a long, gentle slope. To their right, the tall steeple of St. Mary's Catholic Church, built of yellowish "cream brick," reached heavenward in the murky darkness. Now, out of the business district, the car started to descend the little hill, and Johnny and Hazel passed rows of homes, many built with cream brick.

The rough, unpaved road apparently was under construction, which meant that signs were few or even temporarily removed. A few blocks ahead, Johnny needed to turn left to get to the bridge over the Wisconsin River. The steel structure, built in 1906 by the Pan American Bridge Company, replaced a wooden one that had spanned the river for nearly 50 years until a tornado destroyed it in 1905.

But Johnny and Hazel would not reach that steel bridge. Ahead of them lay a pond created decades earlier by a mining company digging clay to manufacture cream brick. In those days, it was known as Armstrong's Clay Hole. No streetlights lit the way. No curb would jolt the car if it missed the turn. And, likely, no street sign told Johnny to turn.

Only two trees stood between the bride and groom—and a watery grave.

II
Farm Family Ties

Henry Peck and son Wallace feed their horse, Peggy, c. 1940. Wallace is Greg Peck's father. Wallace and Greg later tore down the machine shed and granary building behind the barn with nearly tragic consequences.

Zara Peck, Greg Peck's grandmother, poses after Sunday school, c. 1923, with Homer, 2½, and Dorothy, 5. The silo behind them was later torn down. In the background is the original farmhouse.

Harvesting Memories

"I remembered the day I thought my dad had died."

The stones were only an excuse.

"I want to gather some rocks," I told my parents over the phone on that October day in 1997. ". . . for a flower bed."

Sure, I could find interesting, basketball-sized rocks at Stoney Acres, as my mother's brothers dubbed my father's homestead, the one my parents bought from Dad's parents 40 years earlier. But gathering rocks was secondary. What I really wanted to do was say goodbye—goodbye to the farm my parents were selling to the people who'd bought the spread across the road; goodbye to my childhood playground, a rural place for a village kid to explore and discover; goodbye to my heritage.

My parents, Wallace and Marge, bought the Peck farm as newlyweds, intending to live there with my grandparents, Henry and Zara Peck. When the arrangement didn't work out, my parents moved to town, and my grandparents remained on the farm. Grandpa died in the farmhouse at age 83 in 1966, when I was eight years old. Grandma, plagued by osteoporosis, the aftereffects of a broken hip, and later, apparent Alzheimer's, eventually entered a nursing home on the outskirts of Madison, 15 or so miles away. She died there in 1984 at age 96.

After Grandma moved out, renters lived in the farmhouse, and other farmers housed livestock in the barn and tilled the land. But the never-ending upkeep overwhelmed my father, who finally wanted the burden lifted.

Now, as autumn leaves were well into their kaleidoscopic turn, the sale's closing was only a day away. So I hopped into my Ford pickup on that chilly, overcast day and traveled 35 miles from Janesville to Dane County. I cut through my hometown of Marshall and took County T to the little farm. I pulled rubbers over my sneakers, rolled under the electric fence, and headed up the cattle lane behind the aging, white-sided, two-story farmhouse. That's when the memories started flowing back like the stiff autumn wind riffling and rattling through the adjacent stand of mature corn.

I remembered the disarray of chicken coops, sheds, and other farm buildings that once stood on these 40 acres; barbed-wire lanes and rock piles—useless evidence of a hard farm life that somehow, remarkably, raised my dad and five siblings. I recalled helping Dad tear down and burn the tar-papered shacks, each one's demise erasing another otherwise taxable entity; and how an earth-moving company's huge bulldozers buried the rock-strewn fence lines and graded grass waterways—diagonal ribbons across what became one large field.

I recalled how an older cousin, Roger, came one day to help knock down the old block silo, which had stood empty for years, except for pigeons and sparrows. Wielding a sledge, he knocked out tile after colorful tile in a ground-level row until just a few remained. But still, the stout structure wouldn't topple. Someone suggested that the neighbor, Marvin Albrecht, might want to move his new pickup, lest the old gal fall the wrong way.

He did, and it did! The silo snapped power lines and fell in a pile of rubble next to the machine shed, where Marvin's truck had been parked.

I remembered the day I thought my dad had died; the day we were knocking down that huge machine shed, which at one time also housed chickens and served as a granary; it, too, had worn out its usefulness. I walked behind Dad as he cut rafters along the back wall, letting the heavy roof sag down and in. Suddenly, the huge wall toppled on us, pinning my legs in the space between the roof and two studs in the wall. Dad was buried underneath.

"Dad!" I screamed.

"I'm OK," he called, from beneath the rubble.

He had dropped down next to the concrete foundation, and the base of the wooden wall stayed atop it, giving him enough space to breathe and crawl out. He used a pry bar to free me. I shook with fright for the rest of the day.

These and other thoughts filled my mind as I walked along the lane, carrying a pipe I'd found tucked among the cobwebs on a beam inside the old barn. I used the pipe to loosen stubborn stones, which I then tossed along the edge of the manure-filled path. A fox squirrel—fat and sassy from bountiful crops of hickory nuts and corn—bounded along the rocky, wooded fence line, stopping a few feet away. Where was such a critter years ago, when I carried my .22 rifle, I wondered?

Wildlife. I'll never forget the time Dad and I were walking across the farm, probably fixing fence lines, and he suddenly stopped, grabbed Grandma's cocker spaniel, and pointed. There stood the biggest, most majestic whitetail buck I had ever laid eyes on. For a long time, it stood watching us as the dog squirmed in Dad's strong arms.

I strolled down to the back corner, now overgrown with box elders and other scrub trees; to the low land too swampy for crops. I looked skyward and marveled once again at the small but majestic stand of huge oak trees in the farthest reaches of the corner. Across the fence line stood the old Oemig place, where Katie and her four brothers grew up fatherless—their dad dying at a young age in a silo accident. Katie and my brother Tom would attend high school together and eventually walk down the aisle, hand in hand.

I took one last peek inside the 10-foot-by-10-foot metal storage shed our family dubbed "the cabin." I'd built the shed—now dilapidated and rusting, its window smashed—from a kit, with the help of teen buddies. It served as more of a teenage drinking hideout than anything; empty booze bottles—incriminating evidence—likely will forever remain buried next to a nearby ditch.

I walked on, jumping over the rocky fence line to the neighboring property when I found our farmland along the back woods too overgrown with brush, fallen trees, raspberry vines, and velvet weed. When I arrived back at the truck, I unhooked the gate to the electric fence and pulled into the lane to gather the stones. The rocks were neither as colorful nor as interesting as I'd hoped; nicer ones already had found a home in Mom's landscaping in town and decorated sister Karen's yard in Illinois. Still, the load of rocks made my four-by-four sag under the weight.

Back at the white-painted buildings, I took one last look inside the barn. From the lower level, where my grandpa, my father, and his brothers once milked dairy cows by hand, I climbed an aluminum ladder to the haymow. A black cat greeted me as I peered into the mow. I studied the old barn, noticing its cracks and knotholes like never before. I climbed the built-in wooden ladder to the top of the mow, remembering the days I carefully sneaked up those hand-hewed rungs and climbed along the similarly carved beams, playing atop the stacked bales against my father's wishes.

A cow in the barnyard looked up at an open chute, bellowing for a meal. What a neat picture, I thought. I could have kicked myself for not bringing my camera.

I climbed down and took a last look at the pens that once held calves and the stanchions from which cows ate hay and grain, drank from metal cups, and gave up their milk. I examined the farm stuff left for the next owner, claimed a rusty, short-handled shovel, poked my head inside the idle milk house, and then closed the latch to the entrance door for the last time.

I jumped in the truck, glanced across the huge front lawn and saw the big stump to the giant old maple I used to climb—the one a summer storm finally toppled early that year. I recalled the fruit fight I had with a couple of boyhood buddies among the apple trees that once stood in the corner of the massive front lawn. And I remembered the long days of driving a 12-horse Massey-Ferguson lawn tractor on the highway from town to cut grass.

It was then that I knew: I didn't need the camera. I had rocks. And, a few weeks earlier, while helping Dad haul our farm belongings to a storage shed, I laid claim to rusty and worn old tools still tucked away in the barn: a stone puller—a long wooden handle with a C-shaped metal bar that may well have been used to pry loose the stones that were now sitting in my truck; a haystack knife; a wooden hose reel; a garden tiller, and a two-wheeled planter that worked by way of human sweat. These remnants of my heritage were meaningful to me, even if my father had no use for them.

Dad used to state matter-of-factly: "I have no fond memories of growing up on a farm. We didn't have a nickel to our names when we went into town on Saturday nights."

But I loved my memories. As a youngster, after Grandpa had passed on,

I threatened more than once to leave our home in town to go live with Grandma in the old farmhouse.

I loved working with my mom's brother Louie on his farm on the other side of Marshall, the one where the Klecker clan grew up—Mom, Louie, Erv, Roy, Marie, and Fran. I helped Louie in my teen years despite allergies that drove me away for a time. But I returned during summers when I was home from college. I fixed buildings, painted fences and the barn, and—with a face mask and allergy medication—I pulled heavy, green bales off the hay wagon and shoved them down the aluminum chute to the elevator which took them to the mow.

Louie was a good farmer, the kind who did things the right way—keeping his buildings repaired and his machinery dry and in good shape in a huge metal pole shed. He knew he could make a decent living (though one of long days and no vacations) through hard work. Mom says that when three semis pulled up to haul away his milk cows earlier that year, it was the talk of the town.

Another lost dairy farm; another Wisconsin statistic; more lost heritage.

But I have rocks, a few old tools—and pleasant memories. And one other thing—I gleaned a work ethic from my boyhood immersion in farm life. I grew up believing that hard work would bring a good education and, in turn, an honest day's pay. It's a work ethic that seems to be slipping away as each generation is further removed from the family farm; a statistic that no one knows how to measure.

After my dad sold the Peck homestead, these reflections created a backdrop for my thinking as autumn's winds separated the colored leaves from maple, oak, and hickory trees. I believed that, somewhere, somehow, rural Marshall held a story I might feel compelled to tell; one that involved my father and the Peck family, and farm life in Marshall.

But what was it? How would I find it? Where should I look? Little did I know that a tragic story was in front of me. It would require extensive research, and I would begin it without knowing the story's significant links to my life and family heritage; that its re-telling would change the way I thought about Marshall, farm life, and history—forever.

Looking back, I find it shocking that my father could be so fascinated and absorbed by history and yet now know so little about the tragic event that had occurred on that fateful day in September. Granted, the incident happened before he was born. But it happened to the Pirkls, who lived just across the road from where Dad grew up. Dad said that his mother told him the story about Johnny Pirkl while he was still at home, before he married my mother.

"Grandma said it just about killed Grandma Pirkl," Dad said. "My parents never explained why it happened, and I never wondered why. They never tell you anything if you don't ask. It probably came up because of religious conversation."

So my father knew a bit of the story. Yet he'd never heard of "Bridal Pond" until he read about the incident in the *Capital Times*, which printed a fictionalized version of the story. My father saved a copy of Catherine Lazers Bauer's 1980 story.

"That was a complete revelation to me," he said of the story. "When Grandma Peck touched on it, I don't think she said anything about how it happened. Back then, people weren't very interested in family history."

My research would reveal another reason why my father had heard so little about it: The story was so tragic, so painful, that it remained quietly unspoken in the minds and hearts of those who endured it. Yet it remained so etched in the memories of those who tried to make sense of it that survivors would gather 70 years later, in the fall of 1997, to reflect on it, to talk about it, and to mourn once again.

I don't recall the day the idea of telling the story first hit me; but when it did, a nervous excitement set in; an enthusiasm for a story that seemed so compelling and so full of human drama. Yet, it was an endeavor that I wasn't sure I was ready to embark upon, uncertain about my ability and willingness to commit to the challenge.

The project would involve a frank discussion with my fiancee, Cheryl. We were planning a wedding in Hawaii the next May, and without her understanding, acceptance, and support, I had no chance of pulling off the project. We came to a simple and logical agreement: I'd talk to one person—a woman who, by chance, lived in Janesville—to see if she was willing to talk about this painful event. If she wasn't, the idea would die, and the story would remain untold. If she was, it would open the door to a venture I knew would require years of spare time to complete.

I called Joann Ramseier. She was willing to talk.

A Foot in the Door

"You can see I have some trouble with weddings."

The odyssey began with a simple phone call to Joann Ramseier. "My name is Greg Peck. I live in Janesville, and my father is Wallace Peck of Marshall. You know him, don't you?"

"Yes."

I told her I worked for the *Janesville Gazette*, and that I was interested in learning more about her Uncle Johnny and Aunt Hazel because I was considering writing a book about their lives. Joann seemed a bit reluctant, but she agreed to meet with me. She explained how to get to Britt Road, a few miles west of Janesville. On a November evening in 1997, with a bit of snow already on the ground, I pulled my Ford Ranger between the pine trees at the end of the short driveway and parked near the wood-sided house. Joann, her husband, Jim, and Lady, their rambunctious poodle, greeted me at the door. I stepped inside, entering, for the first time, the world of Johnny and Hazel Pirkl.

Joann—the younger of two daughters born to Johnny Pirkl's brother Frank and his wife, Helen—pieced together much of the family tree and history. Joann was born in 1933 on her mother's 34th birthday, so her given name was Helen Joan. Because her name was the same as her mother's, everyone called her Joann for as long as she could remember.

Frank was still running the Pirkl farm when Gov. Warren Knowles honored the family in 1967. Joann brought out a framed photo of the white-haired governor giving her parents a plaque to commemorate the Pirkl place as a Century Farm.

Though Joann wasn't born until nearly six years after Johnny and Hazel were wed, she had heard the stories through the years. "There were some hard feelings about whether or not Hazel would be a suitable wife, and whether Johnny was going to make a good husband. There was obviously some opposition to the marriage by Hazel's side of the family. She turned Catholic, and her folks never attended the ceremony."

The ensuing tragedy left an indelible mark on the Pirkl family. "Our dad never really liked to talk about it," Joann said. "They never talked about the accident; none of my family did, except my mother."

Joann recalled that the tragedy washed away any animosity, any ill feelings between the Pirkls and Fergusons over the marriage. "The families actually became friends. We used to stop and visit with them. It all got worked out."

I found irony in the fact that Joann married someone from Portage, the city where a park contains what became known as Bridal Pond. Jim Ramseier went to school in Portage, when his father was between jobs and the family lived in a summer home on nearby Lake Wisconsin.

Joann was a bit uncertain as to how the pond came to be, or how it relates to the adjacent Wisconsin River. She didn't think it was part of the river, but that river water was channeled in to keep it at a constant level. Portage's famous author, Zona Gale, wrote a fictional short story called "Bridal Pond." But Jim remembered the Portage kids calling it Lover's Pond. However, he admitted, that may have been because it was a favorite spot for young couples to go parking. When they met at UW-Whitewater, Jim asked Joann if she was familiar with Lover's Pond. Joann remembered telling him, "I know all about Lover's Pond."

Joann had fond memories of her grandparents, Joseph and Barbara Pirkl. Johnny's parents worked as a team. "Grandpa never made any decisions on the farm without discussing them with her," Joann said.

After the couple moved to town, Joseph Pirkl still traveled by horse and buggy. The horse, Daisy, came from the farm. "Grandpa got around most of his life by horse and buggy. He used to come out to the farm in his buggy."

Joseph kept that horse in the small barn that stood behind the house, adjacent to Marshall's school grounds. It was the same barn that later would store Johnny's 1927 Chevy. For decades the barn stood on the edge of the sidewalk, so close that grade school kids could reach out and touch it as they passed by on their way to classes. "Grandpa had that car restored, and he learned to drive," she said of Joseph, who was already 67 when Johnny died. "He drove that car," she emphasized, as if the mere notion of keeping and using it was unthinkable.

Joann remembered her grandpa as being very strict. He was straightforward but didn't work as hard at farming as his sons did. His obituary provided more insight: "An active member of St. Mary's Catholic Church, he was respected for his honesty, thoroughness, and a strong determination to stand by the right."

"Grandpa was quite tall and had a white mustache," Joann remembered. "He was always a gentleman."

Barbara Pirkl, on the other hand, was stocky and short. While the couple used an outhouse that stood near the barn at their home in Marshall, they had a wash basin inside. "Grandpa bought a mirror with a medicine cabinet and mounted it so he could see to shave. She could only see the top of her head," Joann said of her grandma. "She always had to wash without looking at herself."

Joann had nothing but respect for her grandmother. "She was the center of the family, very caring, very nurturing. I guess she was one of my favorite people."

Barbara was the sort of family matriarch who fit the image of a farm wife and mother—a hard worker who expected and accepted the role, making sacrifices beyond modern-day comprehension. Sewing and mending clothes were part of the daily ritual. So was firing up the stove with wood to cook for a large family, and baking bread, not buying it; also putting up canned fruit, vegetables, and meat in jars, not going to town to buy food. Laundry? Pump water and fire up the stove again to heat it, as well as the flat iron, and hand-crank the washer. Like most farm wives, the daily grind kept Barbara too busy to have much of a social life, and the lack of transportation further isolated her.

Joann showed me a photo of her Grandma Pirkl standing next to the house in town. She wore a pink dress and held a round, white hat with a flat edge. Behind her, at the corner of the house and next to the outside basement entrance, stands a lush peach tree. Barbara Pirkl obviously had quite a green thumb. She raised six kids mostly on produce harvested from the farm, orchard, and garden. "She started it from a pit," Joann said of the peach tree. "It once got two bushels."

Joseph died in 1944 at age 84. The family buried him in St. Mary's Catholic Cemetery, alongside Johnny and Hazel and little Elleonora, Joseph's youngest, who died in infancy. Joseph's death brought more sorrow to the life of Barbara. It's said that we aren't made to bury our children. But somehow, Barbara gathered the strength to do so more than once. And despite life's trials, tribulations, and heartache, she most often had her chin up.

"Grandma always had such a positive attitude. She never let herself get very down. I stayed with her the summer she had her heart attack," Joann said of the summer of 1947, before Joann entered eighth grade.

"Grandma was such a kind-hearted woman. She stayed with Leonard Springer when he got sick, and with Ed Benesch," Joann said of two of Barbara's sons-in-law. "I always had a lot of respect for her. She saw a lot of heartache. She saw her baby die, Johnny die, and Ed Benesch die."

Mourning came to call again that April day of 1944. Joann remembered being in fourth or fifth grade when her grandpa died. "They said it was stomach ulcers, but it likely was cancer, which they didn't identify as such back then."

According to her obituary, Barbara was at St. Mary's Hospital, Columbus, when God called her in November 1950. She, too, was 84. The obituary named her pallbearers: Charles Langer, Remegius Langer, Charles Doleshal, Arnie Buehler, Frank Motl, and my grandfather, Henry Peck.

"When the goats ran around the yard stiff-legged, we knew it was going to rain."

That's one tidbit Joann remembered about life while growing up on the Pirkl farm.

"We hauled milk to the creamery in Marshall," where the family acquired ice, carved from the frozen Maunesha River, for the icebox and for making ice cream.

The cows grazed down by the marsh, where a windmill provided fresh water. Sod and mint were grown in the marsh, too. Besides dairy cattle, the family raised pigs. The Pirkls grew hay, thrashed grain, raised many vegetables, and had pear and apple trees in a big orchard. "We used to hand-pick sweet corn for sending to a factory," Joann said. They also harvested logs out of the woods on the big hill. The logs were hauled to Marshall, where they were sawn into lumber used for building projects on the farm.

Frank Pirkl's workhorses were his pride and joy, daughter Joann said. He used them to do some road maintenance to reduce his tax bill a bit. "I remember the day he had to put Queenie down," she said of one of her father's favorites. "That was a bad day. She had a tumor on her head; it was choking her off."

Frank tended to invest in his farm, often paying cash for new equipment or buildings instead of taking out loans. Helen wanted to improve the house, but it wasn't until the 1950s that she persuaded him to do so. Their older daughter, Marian, would visit with her own kids and endure the cold, drafty house and lack of indoor plumbing.

During my visit, Joann plugged in a videotape taken around the time the Pirkls finally sold the farm in spring of 1991. It showed many of the buildings looking much as they did decades earlier, when Johnny and Frank farmed the place: cow and horse barns, and a granary, all painted red. The barns had colorful fieldstones cemented into bases that rose nearly head-high. The granary was built as a drive-through for storing the milk wagon. There was a storage area for corn and oats above where the wagon was stored. Frank stored a grinder for producing his own feed up there, Joann explained. The Pirkls used a smokehouse behind the farmhouse to cure ham and bacon. The video shows the farmhouse, built in 1955, that replaced the one in which Johnny and his siblings were raised.

Joann remembered hearing the story of a guy who came around during the Depression with a photo of Johnny and Hazel's wedding. He wanted $35 for it. "That was a lot of money, especially during the Depression. But my dad scraped together some of his last silver dollars to get it. It hung in a prominent place in the new house."

The farmhouse where Johnny and Frank grew up had no running water, just a cistern from which water was pumped into the added-on kitchen. Got an urge? The outhouse was out back. "I can remember that, in college, I brought a city of Chicago girl home and had to tell her how to use the outhouse," Joann reflected.

Floors were slanted in the oldest part of the structure—perhaps because the house may have been moved—and a kitchen and wood storage area were added later. A separate wood shed was out back. A water reservoir in the wood stove provided hot water for cooking, and pails of water for bathing were hauled in from outside and heated on the stove. "We'd bathe in a wash tub in the kitchen," Joann said. "You just hoped no one would walk in while you were bathing. I was the youngest one, so you know who always got the dirtiest bath water."

The old farmhouse was anything but luxurious. "I brought a boy home once, and he listened to the mice running around on the boards above us," Joann said. "I was so embarrassed." The old farmhouse was torn down a year after Joann and Jim married. "They tore down the main part, which was over 100 years old, and kept the kitchen spot. Mom cooked in the kitchen, and the family lived in the old brooder house until the new house was done."

Joann and her husband later moved that brooder house to their 25-acre parcel of land west of Janesville, and it still stands behind the Ramseier home. Joann and Jim figured they'd use the brooder house to raise 300 chickens, just as Joann's parents did, and her grandparents before them. The chicks arrived, but, on the first night, a storm knocked out the power. "We were up all night using lanterns and whatever we could to keep the chicks warm," Joann reminisced. "Mom said, 'Why didn't you just put them back in the boxes they came in to keep warm?' We didn't think of that." While the storm created chaos for Jim and Joann Ramseier, it was nothing compared to one to come.

Joann Pirkl graduated from Marshall High School in 1951 before going to UW-Whitewater. She and Jim Ramseier both started out studying business education, but Jim soon switched majors to become a math teacher. "She asked me to her sorority formal," Jim said, referring to Tri Sigma. Joann explained further: "He was dating my roommate, who was engaged to a guy who was away in the National Guard; he was coming back, so she talked me into going to the sorority formal with Jim. We knew each other because a big bunch of guys and girls would always get together."

Jim had been in the service and avoided going overseas during the Korean War because he played guard and a bit of center for the Atlantic City Naval Air Station's football team. He'd later play center and some wide receiver for Whitewater. Joann graduated in 1955 and Jim in 1956.

Joann and Jim were married, before graduation, in June 1954, at St. Mary's in Marshall, despite the fact that Jim was raised Lutheran. Their marriage was apparently the first mixed-faith ceremony performed in the church; other couples of mixed religions said their vows in the parish rectory, Joann said. Still, the couple exchanged vows outside the church's Communion rail, which, ironically, Joann's Grandpa and Grandma Pirkl had donated to St. Mary's.

Joann had to go to Sunday services that day at Sun Prairie to receive the sacraments before being wed in Marshall. The Marshall church did not have a service that day, perhaps because Father Mark Mueller was rotating services between Marshall and Cottage Grove at the time.

The best man, Jim's brother Gunnar, couldn't sign the marriage license because he wasn't Catholic. So Jim and Joann had one of their ushers sign. Twenty-seven years had passed since Hazel Ferguson defied her parents and turned Catholic to marry Johnny Pirkl at St. Mary's. But, obviously, marriages of mixed faiths still troubled the Catholic church.

Jim and Joann started their teaching careers in Argyle, Jim teaching math and Joann business education. They were two of seven teachers, and Jim was the athletics coach—football, basketball, baseball, and track. Yes, that's two sports in spring. "I'd finish one practice and start the other," Jim said of baseball and track.

Joann took time off when she gave birth to their first child, Renee, in 1956 in Fort Atkinson. The couple ran an insurance agency in Poynette for a couple of years. Then Jim returned to teaching, and they both taught in

Verona schools for years before heading for Janesville in 1965. Jim taught at Janesville middle schools for nearly two decades, then for six years at Craig High School before retiring. Joann didn't work much while they raised their family, but later she spent more than a decade doing data entry for several Janesville companies.

Their first son, Rick, was born in 1959. In the next seven years, Rochelle, Robert, and Roslyn were born. "They're all Rs," Jim joked. Their children attended Hill Crest School, which now stood vacant.

"Johnny was the musician in our family," Joann said. He owned a con-certina—a musical instrument similar to, but smaller than, an accordion. The instrument had buttons rather than a keyboard. Joann told me her daughter Roslyn, a music teacher in Kaukauna, now had it. Johnny also had a windup Victrola with a lift-up top. He played quite a collection of old "78" records. When Johnny died, Joann wound up with the Victrola. But, like Johnny, the Victrola is gone.

In the summer of 1978, Jim's nephew Terry was to be married in Stevens Point, on the same day Joann's niece Nancy was to be wed in Waterloo. Because Terry was an only child and Nancy had lots of siblings, and because Jim and Joann's sons were to be ushers in Terry's wedding, the Ramseiers planned to attend the Stevens Point nuptials. Rob and Rick had gone up a day early for rehearsals. Joann and Jim would thank God they did.

"That night," Joann said, "lightning hit our A-frame house, in the boys' bedroom. The younger girls had practiced going out to the balcony off the bedroom to escape, but they opened their bedroom door, thinking they had to come and get us, and the fire roared in. Rochelle and Roslyn made it out, although a neighbor had to give Roslyn CPR; she wasn't breathing. Renee never made it out, overcome by smoke."

I scanned microfilm at the *Gazette* for more details of the fire that killed Renee and destroyed the family home. In that Saturday's paper, two pictures showed horrific scenes: the peak of the charred A-frame missing, the blackened ruins scattered about the family's front yard. It was stated that Renee, 22, died of heat and smoke inhalation. Roslyn was reported in serious condition at Mercy Hospital, and Rochelle was in fair condition. Neighbors Steve DeForest, his son Chris, and Jeff Krauter had placed a ladder to the second-floor balcony to rescue the two girls. Janesville fire-fighters could see the blazing sky while en route. They donned air masks, but intense heat on the second floor and the "burning inferno" on the lower level kept them from reaching Renee.

Services for Renee, a 1974 graduate of Parker High School, were in St. William Catholic Church. Her sisters were released temporarily from Mercy Hospital to attend. Renee was to have graduated the next fall from Minnesota's Mankato State College with majors in international relations and political science. Renee was buried in Mt. Olivet Cemetery only hours before her parents received notice that she would have graduated cum laude.

Richard Iglar, former assistant principal at Parker High, described Renee as a "quietly efficient girl who was very sharp . . . hard-working . . . and very organized." He applauded her study habits and said she possessed "a brilliant mind" for ambitions dealing with law or diplomatic relations.

"This is a tragic loss," said Richard Windorf, who taught German to Renee in seventh grade. "The world needs more people like Renee Ramseier."

"We would have lost both our boys had they been home, I'm sure, since the lightning hit their bedroom," Joann told me. The Victrola, passed to Joann after her Uncle Johnny died, was destroyed in the fire. "So you can see," Joann said, "I have some trouble with weddings."

Pirkls from Marshall visit Pine City, c. 1936. From left: Frank, daughter Marian, wife Helen, daughter Joann, and Frank's parents, Barbara and Joseph.

Pyburn School, c. 1936. Left: Marvin Albrecht, Dorothy Yelk, Doris Yelk, Bob Walker, Harvey Yelk, Stan Engelke. Middle: Zeno Yelk, Ted Johnson, Stan johnson, Harold (Sterling) Johnson, Francis Engelke, Charles Johnson. Right: Joyce Engelke, Willard Johnson, Elaine Yelk, Marian Pirkl, David Peck. Teacher Viola Martin.

Sisters Act

"Dad talked about crazy things they used to do."

"Johnny was a happy-go-lucky man who enjoyed everything and loved to dance," Marian Zimbric said. Her uncle owned polka, waltz, and hillbilly music records, "Jolly type music. His Victrola was a big, square-type box with a speaker in it."

Marian and Don Zimbric's Waterloo home, on a high lot overlooking the Maunesha River, was a virtual treasure trove of newspaper clippings and Pirkl family photographs. I sat in their house in late November, more than 70 years after Marian's Uncle Johnny wed Hazel Ferguson, recopying stories word for word.

Marian, oldest daughter of Frank and Helen Pirkl, shared memories of the photos—each, seemingly more stunning, and more poignant, than the previous one. A picture of Marian at age two shows her wearing a large, checkered dress. My grandmother, Zara Peck, made the dress, Marian told me. "They used to make things out of nothing. Your grandma made coats and things for me. Some of your family stayed with us after their house fire," she said of a blaze that destroyed my grandparents' home in February 1927.

"We asked them to join us the day of the memorial service," she said, speaking of a more recent event.

Another of Marian's photos shows Frank, Felix Lutz, and Johnny rolling around on the ground, apparently in a wrestling match. Felix has on a black outfit, while the brothers have bib overalls and rolled up shirt-sleeves. They were like "The Three Musketeers," Marian told me. Johnny looks like he perhaps is having the most fun.

Another photo shows Johnny and Frank standing side by side outside the farmhouse. Johnny, a bit shorter than his large-eared, long-armed older brother, holds his hands behind him. Both have slicked-back hair. The white house has a base of fieldstones much like those in the barns. A rain gutter crosses the end of the house, intersecting the lone window. Behind them stand the white smokehouse and, in the background, the outhouse.

One photo shows Johnny hunched over a box camera, snapping a photo. Another, likely taken the same day, shows Johnny sitting on the lawn next to his sister-in-law, Frank's wife. Helen is wearing a light-colored dress; Johnny is wearing his standard—bibs and a shirt with sleeves rolled to the elbows.

The best pictures were yet to come—snapshots of Johnny's gray 1927 Chevrolet. One shows Helen, wearing a plaid dress, sitting on the running board, the car heavily shadowed, appearing black. Standing next to her is Hazel, and the two women have their arms around each other. Hazel is wearing a cardigan sweater, a skirt, and sleek white nylons with dark strapped shoes. Her head is tilted to the side, as if she's looking into a setting sun.

Still another shows Johnny and Hazel seated in the front seat of his prized Chevy, Frank and Felix in back. Hazel is either at the wheel or sitting on Johnny's lap. Her arms are resting on the windowsill; one elbow is on the sill with her hand at the side of her hair—much like a model today might pose to draw attention to her face.

Marian didn't know how long Johnny and Hazel dated. "They probably met at a dance in Sun Prairie," she guessed.

She also didn't know how or where the two became engaged. Marian's family does, however, have the white jewelry box that Johnny gave Hazel for an engagement present. It's shaped like a miniature dresser and has a little mirror and ring handles hanging from its three drawers. Marian gave it to her daughter Jacki, whose husband, Rory Leyden, hoped to refurbish it.

Marian remembered family get-togethers. "The girls would do dishes and talk. Dad talked about crazy things they used to do, and the guys would play horseshoes.

In a playful moment, Frank Pirkl (top), and neighbor Felix Lutz lie atop Johnny Pirkl.

Johnny Pirkl (left) and Frank Pirkl in bib overalls, 1927.

Johnny stooped over, taking a photograph of someone else, 1927.

Helen Pirkl and her brother-in-law, Johnny Pirkl, seated in front of the Pirkl farmhouse, 1927.

"Grandma was a very loving person. She never said a cross word about anybody. She was a typical grandmother in every sense of the word and an immaculate housekeeper.

"Grandpa was kind of a stately person, perhaps six-foot-four-inches," she said. "He always had white hair, as long as I knew him. He was always working out in a workshop at the farm. He'd start up the forge in the morning and build things with iron, make tools; he was always getting metal red hot and bending it. He liked to putter and was always busy. He was a doer. He owned two farms and did the maintenance work on them."

Marian kept the sleigh bells from the Pirkl farm, rescuing them from possible auction buyers just before the farm was sold. The 42 bells, each about the size of a plum, are attached to a circular leather strap that hangs in Marian's basement. She also brought out a little garden hand-hoe with a wooden handle, one of the many things her grandfather fashioned in his workshop.

"He had a clever mind. He would have done well if he'd have gotten out of the farming business."

By age 83, Marian's grandpa suffered from cancer of the esophagus. But that didn't stop him from going out to paint the Wakeman barn in the fall of 1943, just months before his death.

Marian brought out a circa 1932 photo showing the inside of Pyburn School, the same small, country schoolhouse where her father and her Uncle Johnny Pirkl did their readin', writin', and 'rithmetic. The snapshot, full of youngsters wearing smiles and their school-day finest, sat in three rows, filling every desk. The fairly young teacher, Viola Martin, wore a dark dress and stood in back.

Marian knew most of the kids; she was one of them. Among them were Marvin Albrecht, her next door neighbor and the guy who moved his pick-up just before the Peck silo fell; Marian's cousin, Bob Walker; my uncle, David Peck; four Johnson brothers—Stan, Harold, Charles, and Willard; and Zeno Yelk, a kid with a mischievous grin.

Marian remembered the days when boys would come to school after doing barn chores. These days, you'd smell the kid a mile away. Back then, no one batted an eye. Many, perhaps most kids smelled like "farm."

Marian enjoyed classes and knew more about the school than did most kids—her father was clerk of the Pyburn School District. But school wasn't all fun and games for everyone, at least not for that troublemaker, Zeno Yelk.

"He kept having the teacher break her ruler across his knuckles. But it just never sunk in. One time, he had an ax on the roof and was pretending he was a fireman and was going to chop a hole in the roof. They had to call my dad."

My plan for February 1999 seemed like a logical one—get Joann Ramseier and her sister, Marian Zimbric, together to reminisce and perhaps feed off each other's memories. But their cousin Jim Benesch threw a bit of caution my way. He didn't think they got along so well and said they'd had a dispute over the sale of the Pirkl farm. I called Joann anyway, bringing up the question about a disagreement with Marian over the sale of the farm.

"She wanted to sell it for a lot less than we ended up selling it for," Joann said. "She worked with a real estate agent out of Waterloo, and I guess I didn't like, not so much the way he was doing it, but one of his employees.

"It's a long story. I had some problems with a renter we had there. She was taking care of things," Joann said of her sister, "and, from a distance, I just didn't agree with the way things were done. But that's all pretty much past us. Maybe when you're a little farther away, you see things you don't see when you're right on top of them."

So we chose a day to meet and headed for Marshall in the Ramseiers' Ford Taurus. Jim drove while I asked Joann questions. We took back roads through Fulton and Utica, routes I'd never traveled before.

"Your grandma told my mother the best way to get down to Janesville from Marshall after we moved here," Joann said of Zara Peck.

Joann recalled a humorous story her father told of his dating days, before he started courting her mother. He'd taken a girl out with his horse and buggy, dropped her off afterward, and then headed for home. But he fell asleep en route. Frank awoke to find that the horse had delivered him to a previous girlfriend's house.

Joann told of faint memories of her Uncle Ed's visits and of trips to Pine City. "Uncle Ed used to come down on the train once in a while; the women came down to visit after Uncle Ed passed away. They lived in rather impoverished conditions. Their farmland was not good. They didn't make much money. My aunt would walk quite a distance to church every morning. Our family sent clothes for their kids after they had a house fire. Instead of making use of them, she donated them to the Catholic church. That's just the way she was.

"Uncle Ed had a gander that loved to chase me. They had an outhouse. I was afraid to go to the outhouse because the gander would stand and wait for me."

Joann said her family went to visit in 1936 and again in 1937 to attend a Hady funeral, when Joann was about four years old. "I was the littlest, so I had to crawl behind the coffin to unplug a lamp. I had nightmares about that, that I woke up and heard the person laughing."

Joann remembered hearing stories about her Minnesota cousins Dorothy and Bernadine when they attended nursing school in St. Paul. Dorothy was rather wild and joined the girls in a corner room, where they'd sneak away to smoke—something girls just didn't do in those days. She was almost expelled.

But Dorothy joined the convent, and Bernadine worked at a Catholic girls school in St. Paul. Neither one learned how to drive, which made it rather amusing when they went to a dealer to buy a car. They had to ask how to drive it before heading off down the road.

Joann and Marian told a heartbreaking tale of their parents' final years. Helen was sickly much of her life, apparently having been affected by rheumatic fever at a young age. Later, she suffered from diabetes and a series of heart attacks, spells that wearied her husband. Frank, apparently a bit of a drinker earlier, found brandy too hard to resist, too easily used to numb the pain, the frustration, and the sorrow.

When Helen died at Columbus Hospital in 1975, Frank was a patient there, too. Eventually, medical personnel helped wean him to two shots of brandy per day. He spent four years at the Jefferson County Home before moving to a small apartment building around the corner from Marian's home in Waterloo. From there, he'd walk over for a meal and a visit nearly every day. But in July 1982, Marian's daughter Jacki went to visit her grandfather and to retrieve his laundry. Frank went to the refrigerator, but when he reached out his arm, he couldn't make it function. Jacki called her mother, who hurried over.

Frank had suffered a stroke, which left him using a walker and unable to speak or swallow food well. He moved to Willows Nursing and Rehabilitation Center in Sun Prairie. He wouldn't use pictures to communicate, Marian remembered. She recalled the time she stopped in, and he was all excited about a previous visitor. All she could make out was "Main Street." Marian started naming everyone she could think of on Main Street but was not able to understand him.

Frank died in April 1984, 21 months after his stroke. At his funeral, Marian talked to Bud Herman of Marshall, who told her how he'd recently taken his father, Ed—who many years earlier was left crippled after being caught in a power-takeoff shaft on the side of a manure spreader—to visit Frank. Frank, of course, had been excited to see Ed, and that's who he was trying to tell Marian about.

Marian and Joann recalled that mice invaded the Pirkl farmhouse, especially in winter. They were attracted to the seed corn that Frank stored in an unused bedroom upstairs. The girls set mousetraps, using cheese or peanut butter for bait, and one time they each caught two in a single trap.

"We used to have a catching contest and get paid so much per mouse," Marian said. "The best mouse catcher was whoever reset their traps the most often."

"We'd set them and listen for the traps and run up to see who caught one," Joann said. "We had cats all over the farm; we should have had one in the house. But you didn't have cats in the house in those days."

Marian and Joann spent days playing on the flatbed hay wagon. They used it as a performance stage, or they stacked wooden crates on it to form a playhouse. The two would mimic the country-western singers they heard on Chicago radio station WLS. "We'd stand on the hay wagon and pretend we had guitars and entertain," Marian said.

"My favorite song was 'Red Sails in the Sunset,'" added Joann, who remembered entertaining her father and his hired hands by singing in the barn.

One time, their father had hitched his team of horses to the wagon while the girls were playing house. Suddenly, the wind toppled the crates that formed their refrigerator, and the startled horses bolted. Fortunately, no one was hurt.

The girls would wait until the cows left the barn. Then they would lay boards across the manure gutters, so they could race their coaster wagons. Each girl would sit on one leg in the wagon and use the other leg to propel it around the barn. "We had good times until we forgot to take the boards out one time and Dad let the cows in and the boards got all squirted," Joann said.

In the summer, Frank would clean out the pigpen—the little, white shed that stood north of the big barn—and the girls used it to play grocery store with neighbor kids. They'd save empty cereal boxes and stock shelves with brand-labeled canned goods that had been opened from the bottoms, giving the look of unopened store goods. "We'd sell your dad stuff with play money," Marian said. "That was a big time when your dad came up."

"I used to love the winter. We had little skis, and we'd ski all over the fields."

The sisters also told about the winter when my dad sprained his ankle while skiing down the big hill with them. Dad also got hurt one year while sledding, running into a wooden gate at the base of the hill.

Marian told of the time, just before her New Year's Eve date, that she was sledding down the hill and fell off, skinning her chin, nose, and cheek. Her date, no doubt, was less than pleased. That jogged Joann's memory of the day she was riding with a girlfriend on her bike, heading down the gravel drive, when the friend started wiggling on the back, and Joann lost control and tipped over. "I skinned my whole face. We had to go to Madison East to get our eighth-grade diplomas, and no one wanted to stand by me; they thought I had some disease. I was picking gravel out of my knee for a week."

The two recalled a time when they were younger and Joann, who Marian said was the cuter one with the curly hair, thought it'd be fun to pick up handfuls of hay dust and dump it on her head. "Dad, or the hired hand, called her 'Dusty,' and she started to cry, and the tears turned the dust to mud all over her face," Marian chuckled.

It wasn't all fun and games. Frank once had a hired hand who fancied himself as a bit of a cowboy, lying atop a horse and strumming his guitar. "When Dad let him go, he was so mad he said he was going to kidnap me,"

Hazel Ferguson (standing) and Helen Pirkl in front of Johnny Pirkl's Chevy, outside the Pirkl farmhouse, 1927.

Johnny Pirkl and Hazel Ferguson in the front seat of Johnny's prized 1927 Chevrolet. In the back seat are Frank Pirkl and Felix Lutz.

Joann said. "So Dad drove us to school after that."

The girls recalled picking cucumbers in the garden and pushing the hand mower around the lawn. Their father never mowed until he bought a power rider many years later. "We'd mow about an acre and a half," Marian said. "We had to take turns; one person couldn't do it all at once. It was a big deal when we finally got a push mower with rubber tires.

"We were never bored. I don't understand it. 'We're bored; there's nothing to do'— that's all you hear from the grandkids these days."

Marian Pirkl graduated from Marshall High School in 1948, attended Madison Business College for a semester, then took a job with Hartford Insurance in Madison for a year. She and Don Zimbric married in St. Mary's Catholic Church in 1950. Marian told of the rocky start to their courtship.

"He made quite a name for himself as a baseball pitcher," she said of the Waterloo native. Marian and two girlfriends watched Marshall play football in Deerfield one fall, then dropped in on the Waterloo homecoming dance. Don asked Marian to dance several times. Then he asked to drive her home. "I said 'I came with the girls, and I'm going home with the girls.'"

One of those friends was Jean Herman. A few weeks later, Jean called, saying she had a date and wanted Marian to accompany them as a blind date with Don. She agreed, but not too willingly. "I was not too nice to him, he being from Waterloo and me being from Marshall," she said of the rival villages. "I was young; I was a brat, let's face it. He walked me to my door that night and said, 'You make me so damn mad, I'm going to marry you someday.'"

Don was starting a 45-year career at the malt factory in Waterloo, and Marian quit her insurance job shortly after getting married. The couple lived in a poorly maintained house on the hill on Marshall's Main Street for awhile before moving to Waterloo.

It was good that Marian quit working after wedding Don. She was already expecting. Their first child, Greg, was born in July 1950. More would soon follow. Gary was born in 1951, Gail in 1953, Nancy in 1957, Karen in 1961, Dan in 1962 and Jacki in 1966. Between them, they have given Marian and Don 18 grandkids and one great-grandchild.

Joann and Marian rifled through a cardboard box of family papers and documents.

One item showed the funeral expenses for Katherine Hady, their great-grandmother. Frank Scheiber, undertaker, embalmer, and funeral director from Watertown, charged $60 for the casket. After adding the embalming, teams of horses, wagons, and other expenses, son-in-law Joseph Pirkl Jr. was left to pay the grand total of $100.

Another paper showed Joseph Pirkl in 1923 as administrator of the estate of Frank Hady, their great-grandfather. Still another listed a $1,175 mortgage, with seven percent interest, which Frances Pirkl took out on the Pirkl farm in 1868, payable to Watertown's John Duscheck—now spelled Dushack.

Joann found the paperwork detailing her Uncle Johnny's estate. It showed he had a net worth of less than $4,000. Less about $665 for the executors, or lawyers, his family received the remaining $3,300, or so.

Also in the box was the marriage license for Johnny and Hazel, the document that had been altered to correct the bride's and groom's signing on the wrong lines.

Uncle Johnny Pirkl with Bob and Dorothy Walker up in a tree, 1927.

The Flower Girl

"I can still see him sitting there on that stool."

More than 70 years had passed since Johnny and Hazel had made wedding plans. But Dorothy Voelker could relive one scene as if it were only yesterday. She remembered the day she piled into Johnny's car with Johnny and her mother, Alta. They were headed to Madison, where Johnny intended to buy his five-year-old niece, Hazel's flower girl, a dress for the upcoming nuptials.

"He picked out the dress," Dorothy recalled. "A lady tried it on me and put the headpiece on—it had rhinestones and two little doves, the doves having a silver outline and the rhinestones inside them. My mom thought it was too much money. But Johnny said, 'That's just what I want her to look like.' I can still see him sitting there on that stool."

Hazel, who was handy with needle and thread, stitched a little green pillow with white lace circles to match the dress. "I carried the rings down the aisle on the pillow," Dorothy said with a glimmer in her eye.

More than 70 years later, she still had the dress, though the decades had left it faded and discolored in spots. The pillow also had faded, and the stitched seam in back had pulled apart. The bracelet little Dorothy wore during her Uncle Johnny's wedding was still shiny. It was adorned with amethyst, or violet quartz, and each silver section was decorated with an intricate design. The bracelet was a gift from Ida Ferguson, mother of the bride.

In 1998, Dorothy Voelker and her husband, Bud, lived in an attractive, 1½-story home just off Capitol Drive, a main thoroughfare in the Milwaukee suburb of Brookfield. I visited them on a snowy day early that year. Birds dined at a Green Bay Packer feeder in the front yard. Several pieces of older furniture graced the comfortable living room where we talked.

Before we started chatting, Dorothy had a surprise for me. I did not know that her mother and my grandmother, Zara Peck, were friends— good friends.

Dorothy handed me three identical pieces of paper. The first said, "Alta from Henry and Zara and all the kiddies." The other two pages contained a poem that my grandmother had written to accompany the gift that Zara and Henry Peck gave to Alta and Ed Walker on their wedding day:

> *When you are married and there is just you two,*
> *Here's a bright new kettle to cook you a stew.*
> *Put in some beef or a chicken or two,*
> *Some vegetables and spice; and I think it will do.*
> *To keep your man's love always whole,*
> *Be very sure to keep his stomach full.*
> *Cake and puddings, stews, and pies,*
> *And he'll laud his Alta to the skies.*
> *So, dear Alta girl, Be sure on your mettle,*
> *Best wishes to you with this bright new kettle.*

The letter continued in attractive, cursive handwriting:

> *Sincerely, with all best wishes for every future happiness for you and your husband. Thanking you for the many acts of kindness you have done for us.*

> *We remain,*
> *Sincerely, your friends,*
> *The whole Peck family*

Two more scraps of paper contained yet another poem to Alta, this one from Margaret Calkins Cast, my Grandma Zara's sister:

Joy to the bride, God bless her,
So winsome and jolly, and sweet.
Always dressed so becoming,
And a lady from head to feet.
Alta the bride of the moment,
And a treasure for any young man.

They say they all call him a Walker,
But some of the time, I'll bet he ran.
Now boys, we'll leave this to your judgment,
Could you get a bride half as sweet.
You sure would get in a hustle,
And not stand around on your feet.
May the trials of life scarcely touch her,
But continue bright all the way.
May every dawn be as rosy,
As it was on her wedding day.

Sincerely, Margaret Calkins Cast.

Bob Walker, Dorothy's younger brother, remembered much about growing up on a farm during The Great Depression: The holidays, the neighborliness, and the hard work.

Bob shared some of those memories in December 1997 while sitting in the kitchen of his home on County TT, within eyesight of the farm Johnny and Hazel planned to call home. Bob's father, Edward, bought the Walker place in 1944, and Bob and his wife, Ramona, bought it from Ed around 1960. As we discussed the changes in ownership, Bob shared another piece of information regarding my heritage, one that I'd heard but forgotten in my younger years, when such details meant little to me: My Grandpa Henry Peck's father, Milton, once owned the farm where we were now visiting together.

Edward Walker came from Hillsboro, another small town about 50 miles northwest of Madison, but not before he survived a bout with appendicitis in 1915. "A doctor came from Milwaukee by train, and they operated on him right on the kitchen table," Bob said.

Johnny Pirkl, though only 18, stood up as best man when his sister Alta married Edward Walker in 1920 at St. Mary's. The couple raised three children. Dorothy was born on July 21, 1922. Bob was born in 1924, and Kenny arrived much later, in 1940. Before buying the Milton Peck place on County TT, and except for a brief stay on a farmstead south of Waterloo—the reason behind it lost through time—the family lived on a farm on Highway T. It was less than a mile walk to Pyburn School. It was another mile or so farther to the Pirkl farm. The short hop from the Pirkl place made it easy for Dorothy's Uncle Johnny to visit.

"He'd always play with us kids, always coming to our farm to spend time there," Dorothy said. "Mom and him were quite close. He'd drop in every week or so."

Dorothy has several photos taken in the spring of 1927. One shows Johnny and Alta sitting near a stump outside the Walker farmhouse. Johnny is dressed in a black suit and pants; Alta is wearing a dress with small checks. The picture shows the brother and sister grinning and hugging tightly, as if hanging on for dear life.

Johnny Pirkl and Hazel Ferguson
up in a tree.

Johnny Pirkl hugs his sister Alta Walker in spring 1927, in front of Walker home on County T.

Hazel Ferguson and Alta Walker pose with Alta's kids, Dorothy and Bob, at the Walker farm in spring 1927.

Another shows Johnny and Hazel sitting among the bare branches atop a moderate-sized tree. Johnny wears the same outfit; Hazel is in a printed dress and sandal shoes. A similar snapshot shows Dorothy in a white, knee-length dress on the second rung of a ladder leading to the treetop. Johnny sits near the top of the ladder, holding his little nephew Bob on his lap.

"Johnny always would play with us kids on the front lawn," Bob recalled of those days when he was just three years old. "He'd climb up the small trees, and he'd grab us kids, and we'd sit with him up there."

A fourth photo shows Hazel and Alta smiling and squeezing into a child's wooden, metal-wheeled wagon. Little Dorothy and Bob are in front. It appears they are getting ready to be pulled.

"My mom was so happy because Johnny and Hazel were going to be so close by," Dorothy said of the couple's plans to farm the Wakeman place on Highway TT.

Bob Walker recalled that his Uncle Frankie was a nice man. "I always got along with him real well," said Bob, a slender man with dark hair. "Whatever I did was OK, and whatever he did was OK with me. He was a jolly guy, too."

Maybe some of that jolliness, that fun-loving nature, rubbed off on Bob from Uncle Johnny and Uncle Frankie. Bob related a mischievous prank from his younger days. "We'd spread Limburger cheese on the manifold of a Model T. That stunk something terrible when the guy would go to take his gal home."

Dorothy and Bob described their parents as admirable people, unafraid of work. "Mom was hard-working; a wonderful mother; good homemaker; good cook; could sew," Dorothy said. "Most farm women were good homemakers."

Alta Walker was a stout woman with black hair and a round face. Her dark eyes balanced a pointy nose. She was a pretty lady who liked clothes and always dressed neatly. "Mom was an awful nice gal, kind-hearted, like the rest of the Pirkls," Bob said. "The work the mothers used to have, pressing white shirts with an iron heated on the wood stove. How much wash those women went through!"

Those were the days when a washer had a pump handle to turn the agitator, and the women would wring the clothes by hand. It was a tedious, time-consuming task. But Alta Walker somehow made her way through the daily chores with time to spare. "She always had time for other people, too, if they needed help," Bob said.

"She could play the piano by ear," Dorothy told me. "She never took lessons; she was just pretty musical." On the keyboard, Alta Walker played such songs as "The Bells of St Mary's," "Anchors Away," and, ironically, "When Johnny Comes Marching Home."

Edward Walker was nice looking, too. Dorothy showed a photo of a handsome man, his blond hair combed up, his eyes attractive. He was a taller man, perhaps six feet, but his shoulders rounded later in life. "I always got along good with him," Bob said. "He was a kind-hearted guy, too. He liked to be in different things."

"He loved to talk to people," Dorothy said. "He was a 'people' person. That's why he served on the town and county boards."

Dorothy produced an obituary for her father, who died in 1968 at age 76 at Columbus Hospital. It said he'd lived near Marshall since 1915. He was a member of St. Mary's Church and its Holy Name Society. He served on the Sun Prairie Town Board for 23 years and, at one point, was town chairman. He was a Dane County Board supervisor for 17 years and a former member of the Dane County Parks Commission.

Edward Walker also was a director of Medina Mutual Insurance, a company still in existence. My mother used to work there part time. Records listing officers show that her brother, my Uncle Erv Klecker—who died of cancer in 1996—served separate stints as president and secretary. They also reveal that Joe Pirkl served as vice president from 1938-1942.

Alta R. Walker lived to be 82, dying at a Sun Prairie nursing home March 16, 1982. She, too, was active in St. Mary's church and its Altar Sodality. She's buried in the church cemetery.

While relics of history remain at Hazel Ferguson's Gaston School, today commuters and farmers alike pass by the former site of Pyburn School without giving it a thought. Most are unaware that, decades ago, a country schoolhouse sat on the big curve where Highway T and TT briefly intersect before again cutting across farm fields.

But Dorothy Voelker remembered the one-room grade school. "The teacher was strict," Dorothy said. "They certainly got learning done. When she said 'jump,' you said 'how high?' Nobody seemed to get out of line."

A potbelly stove sat in the back, but it barely kept the schoolhouse warm enough for students to concentrate. Kids had to lug in firewood. The girls wore dresses and, in winter, snow pants, often leaving them on during classes on cold days. "Once, on a cold, snowy day, we got there, and the teacher had dropped the key on her way to the school," Dorothy recalled. "Some boys opened a window, and my brother Bob, being the smallest boy, was boosted through it to open the door from inside."

While kids those days wore rubbers or overshoes for doing barn chores, the girls wore clunky oxford shoes to school, keeping a second pair of shoes for Sunday church. Dorothy recalled that her mother made all her school dresses. "That's why going with Johnny and buying one for the wedding was such a big deal."

After Dorothy's years in the elementary Pyburn School, she went on to Medina Free High School, where she met Lyle Voelker; "Bud," they called him.

"People have called me Bud since I was this high," he said, holding his hand about as high as mature alfalfa. "I never liked the name Lyle. Everyone called me Bud—except my English teacher. She called me Lyle."

Bud, a lefty, was fast on his feet on the basketball court, playing forward and making all-state for his scoring ability in his junior year. He also played first base on the Marshall baseball team sponsored by Lazers Motors.

"We were both in the school band," Dorothy explained. "I played the French horn, and Bud played sax."

Dorothy was also a cheerleader and performed in school dramas. Their spots in the band gave Bud the opening he needed. "He manipulated it after a marching band tournament at the Capitol Square so I had to ride home with him in his car," recalled Dorothy, who explained that no buses were available to cart kids to such functions at that time. "He took me to a movie in Madison, and we started dating after that."

She couldn't remember the movie, but the fellow obviously made a lasting impression. Bud graduated in 1939; Dorothy in 1940. They wed

August 2, 1941, at St. Mary's. After he finished technical school and a stint in the Navy, Bud got a job at Evinrude Outboard Marine, and he and Dorothy moved to the Milwaukee area, where the couple raised two children, Janet and Dick. They now have four grandchildren.

Bud was a handsome, slim man with a moderately dark complexion. An attractive crop of white hair framed his face, and wire-rim glasses rested on his nose. When he stood to shake my hand, I noticed that, somewhere along life's perilous road, he'd lost his right thumb.

Dorothy kept her blond hair at modest length and wore makeup and lipstick. She obviously pays careful attention to her appearance.

Decades later, Dorothy still recalled thinking about Johnny and Hazel on her own wedding day. "They cross my mind a lot of times, and I don't think I ever see a wedding that I don't think about that."

"I remember waving goodbye when they left," Bob said of Johnny and Hazel's honeymoon trip, "and Grandma Pirkl saying, 'They never should leave in this terrible fog.'"

Bob's young age saved him from much of the heartache others endured. It only truly hit home for Bob 70 years later, in the fall of 1997, when family and friends gathered at St. Mary's for a service to reflect, talk, and mourn once again.

"You're busy through the years and don't think about it. The service sure brought back a lot of memories and years. The day of the anniversary ceremony, we spent all afternoon out here looking at pictures, talking about things, after we ate at the Cobblestone."

During the service, Bob gazed past the altar and through a special window, a tribute to Johnny and Hazel Pirkl. "I'd look at that window in church, and I'd picture the whole thing. The whole town was shocked."

Johnny's Date

"Johnny and I went to places like the Golden Lantern in Bristol."

Sue Woerpel, whose real name is Catherine, was a sister to Bill Hamshire, pallbearer for Johnny Pirkl. Sue remembered a key detail about Johnny Pirkl. "My sister Ella, who's 91, used to go with him," she said.

Ella Fullert lived at Sun Prairie Health Care Center on West Main Street in Sun Prairie. I told Sue that I'd be very interested in visiting with Ella to learn what she might remember about Johnny. I asked her to tell Ella that I'd visit her in a week or so and to explain why I'd be interested in speaking with her.

One week later, in March 1998, I pulled into the paved parking lot at the one-story nursing home. I asked to speak with Mrs. Fullert, and a woman directed me to the lounge area, where residents were finishing breakfast and awaiting a religious program.

Even at 91, Ella Fullert was a nice-looking woman. I could imagine back 70-some years and understand why Johnny Pirkl had been attracted to her. I introduced myself, crouching down next to her wheelchair as she sat sipping coffee. She seemed skeptical of my intentions.

"I don't want my name in any old book," she said. I continued to ask questions, however, and she provided some answers. "I was doing housework for Alta Walker when I was in my teens," she said of Johnny's sister. "I went from one place to the other when a family had a baby. They needed help. It wasn't very profitable. I was there a couple of months when Bob Walker was born."

I remembered how Dorothy Voelker, Bob's older sister, told me that Johnny was quite close to Alta. Apparently, during one of Johnny's visits to his sister's farm, he met the young Ella Hamshire. Ella told me that Ed Walker, Alta's husband, was her cousin. "You had to work as a teen-ager back then. That was the only work I could get. I house-kept for cousins when they had babies."

Ella then told me what she remembered about Johnny Pirkl. "Johnny was nice. . . . We just ran around together. We went to barn dances. He was a very nice person. We went together for the summer, and then he went his way, and I went mine. There were no hard feelings."

By the time Johnny wed Hazel, "I'd been working at a shoe factory in Watertown for two years," Ella said. "Johnny and I were friends then. We talked, but I didn't go to his wedding."

The religious program had started. A woman was speaking from the front of the lounge area. Another elderly lady seated nearby asked us to "sshhhh" so she could hear. It wasn't the best place to conduct an interview. But Ella continued talking about Johnny.

"Johnny and I went to places like the Golden Lantern in Bristol, to Clyman, and to Weisensel's on the north side of Sun Prairie. We were good dancers—waltz, polka, square dances. They'd get an orchestra together."

Ella joined her sister Sue and her parents at the wake for Johnny and Hazel. "It was the first time I ever saw Hazel," she said. "I feel real bad that that happened to him because he was a nice person. It was in the evening, and lots of people were there. I feel bad about it every time I think about it. Someone like him shoulda never died that way."

Ella eventually married Jerome Fullert in Rockford, Illinois. "Jerome and I went to Rockford because it was cheap and quick to go there. We'd gone to catechism instruction together, but I never dreamed we'd end up together. We went 'off and on' for years. I quit work after getting married."

A month or two after our brief chat, I sent Ella a letter, hoping to glean more details about Johnny Pirkl. But a few days later, my letter came back unopened, stamped "Return to Sender." In handwriting were the words "Not at this address."

I questioned this and called Ella's sister Sue to explain that my letter had been returned, unopened. Sue told me that Ella had died.

Ella A. Fullert, age 91, died April 15, 1998, at Sun Prairie Health Care Center, according to her obituary. She was born October 10, 1906, in the town of Medina, to John and Catherine (Kohout) Hamshire. She married Jerome A. Fullert on May 22, 1928. Jerome died in 1990. The couple had no children of their own.

"Mrs. Fullert was a lifelong area resident where she was employed seasonally at the Wisconsin Cheeseman in Sun Prairie. She was a member of St. Jerome Catholic Church, Columbus."

The obituary stated that besides her brother Walter and sister Catherine (Sue), she was survived by a nephew, Erwin (Elinor) Johnson of Janesville; and two nieces, Sally (Victor) Martin of Marshall and Beatrice (Willard) Borchert of Sun Prairie, all of whom Ella and her husband raised from childhood.

I wondered about this, so once again I called Sue. She explained that the couple had parented three nieces and a nephew. One niece, Marie, died about a year before Ella passed away. Ella's sister Mary and her husband, Andrew, had four children. Mary spent time in a sanitarium with tuberculosis. She recovered enough to return home, only to be fatally stricken during a 1932 flu epidemic. Two years later, Andrew died in an auto accident, and the four children became orphans. Ella and Jerome, who lived in Deansville, and Ella's parents, who lived on the Hamshire homestead, shared the responsibility of raising the children.

I had one personal question for Sue. Did Ella and Jerome not have children of their own because they suddenly had a house full of nieces and a nephew? "No, Ella couldn't have children," her sister said.

Though I only met with Ella Fullert one time, I was able to imagine what a good mother she would have been.

Cast of "Lighthouse Nan" outside Bristol Dance Hall. From left: Sylvester Janisch, Leon Benesch, Emma Blaschka, Verona Baker, Bill Hamshire, Lucille Hebl (hidden), Grace Langer, Alvin Benesch, Felix Lutz, Olive Baker, Johnny Pirkl and Bernadine Plachy.

Part of the cast of "Lighthouse Nan" posing outside the dance hall. From left: Sylvester Janisch, Verona Baker, Bill Hamshire, Grace Langer, Leon Benesch, Olive Baker, Johnny Pirkl, Felix Lutz.

Principled Principal

"Hazel's mom went to the wedding."

Every news article, and almost every person I interviewed, indicated that Hazel Ferguson's parents, Ida and John, did not attend their daughter's wedding because they objected to her marriage to Johnny Pirkl. But Jim Langer believed otherwise.

"Hazel's mom went to the wedding," he said in February 1998. "Hazel's dad didn't."

Jim was born May 27, 1911. That made him 16 when he attended the wedding in which his cousin, Cyril Langer, stood up as best man. At age 86, Jim was one of the few living witnesses to the ceremony. My former principal at Marshall Elementary School wore bifocals and used a walking cane to steady his slow and shaky steps. But his mind was sharp. It's not unusual that facts and details would fill the head of a former educator.

Apparently, Ida slipped inside the church as the bridal couple took their places at the front. Few people saw her come in. But Jim Langer, sitting in the back, noticed her. Her husband, John, likely brought her to church and waited outside in the car, Jim surmised. As soon as the ceremony ended, Ida slipped out.

Jim's parents, Remegius and Amelia, lived on the farm that was later occupied by the William Pautsch family. Despite the fact that my father loved local history and was born on the Peck farm across County T from the Pautsch farm, he did not know that the Langers had once lived there.

My father also was unaware of the fact that Jim Langer had a sister, Grace, who was about five years older than Jim. Grace was born on the farm over the hill from the Pirkl place. By the time Jim was born, the Langers had moved to the town of York.

"The Langers and Pirkls were good friends. They came to our place a lot," Jim said of the Pirkl family's visits to the Langer farm in York. "Joseph Pirkl drove up in a horse and buggy, and later in Johnny's car."

Marian Zimbric had several photos that prompted a second visit to Jim. One snapshot, she believed, showed a couple of fellows dressed in odd costumes at a masquerade party. Two others showed faded lineups of young people dressed up: ladies, in dresses, some with hats; guys with white shirts, sweaters, or suit coats.

Marian was certain that one photo showed her Uncle Johnny, dressed in shiny shoes, dark slacks, a wrinkled but bright white long-sleeved shirt, and a stubby, dark bow tie. He stood—belt pulled high at the buckle, hands cupped behind him—next to Felix Lutz. Felix had a dark suit coat that matched his slacks. His colorful tie was hanging out, partially covering his white shirt that needed a bit more tucking in. Felix had his hands at his side. His already-receding hairline made his ears look even bigger. The people in the two photos appeared to be standing on a dirt road. In one photo, an old-time car—perhaps a soft-top—was parked behind them; the corner of a building was visible in the background.

When he saw the photos, Jim Langer asked his wife, Lucille, to retrieve a box from their basement. Meanwhile, he sat at the kitchen table and started naming each person.

But how could he, after all these years, be so certain? Lucille soon arrived with a box full of evidence—memorabilia from the life of Grace Langer. Jim said he thought of tossing the contents in the fireplace years ago. Fortunately, he did not. In the box was a program from a play, "Lighthouse Nan," performed in 1925. The photos showed the cast.

"A year before Johnny and Hazel were married (actually two years), the Catholic Order of Foresters gave a play," Jim explained. "Johnny was in it.

Hazel would come along and watch them practice. They gave it at the old town hall and practiced there, too."

The program spells out the parts of the play in simple form:

Act 1: Interior of lighthouse, Carolina coast, Nan begins her education.

Act 2: Same scene, ten years later; Nan continues her education.

Act 3: Library in John Enlow's home, two years later; Nan completes her education.

The program also provided the roles of each performer:

Sylvester Janisch was the Honorable John Enlow, president of Seacoast Banking Company.

Bill Hamshire was Ned Blake, his private secretary.

Leon Benesch was Ichabod, the old keeper of the lighthouse.

Johnny Pirkl was Sir Arthur Choke, a British aristocrat.

Felix Lutz was Injun Jim, "a bad man."

Verona Baker was Nan, "a little roustabout."

Grace Langer starred as Moll Buzzer, "a gentle antelope."

Lucille Hebl was the Honorable Sarah Chumley Choke, Arthur's sister.

Olive Baker was Hortense Enlow, a city belle.

Emma Blaschka directed the play.

Bernadine Plachy, who was about 16 years old, was the pianist.

A snapshot of Grace Langer and Leon Benesch in costumes was among the contents in the box—Grace as Moll Buzzer, and Leon as the hen-pecked husband with a beard. Some photos were identical to Marian Zimbric's. "They were taken outside the dance hall at Bristol, across from the Bristol Church," Jim said. "We used to call it 'The Vestibule to Hell' because you could buy moonshine liquor across from the church."

Jim Langer, who seemed to be a stern, no-nonsense principal at Marshall Elementary and Junior High from 1963 until his retirement in 1977, hid a humorous streak.

Because we had lived on the same block as the Langers, I wondered why my father did not know about Jim's older sister. I learned that she had died when Dad was very young.

Jim then pulled out a photo showing Grace and two youngsters in front of a two-door 1929 Chevy. Grace earned a teaching degree from

Whitewater Normal School and later taught at Maple Center School in rural York.

The Langer farm was equipped with a system of batteries that generated electricity for the barn and house. Jim described the batteries as a wall of glass jars filled with cells and acid. An engine recharged them. A Sun Prairie businessman by the name of Thompson had installed the system, but a part was missing. He had recently moved to a new home. When Grace and her mother attempted to pick up the missing part—Grace driving the 1929 Chevy—they realized they did not know where he lived. They stopped at a meat market to get information on his whereabouts, but no one knew.

"He used to live across the railroad tracks," Jim said. "Pa said, 'Don't go across the tracks because Thompsons don't live there anymore.' Grace said, 'OK.' Talk about the hands of fate. They went to ask the new people who lived in Thompson's old house where he'd moved to."

The tracks ran parallel to a shed at the stockyards. On their way back from the former Thompson home, they met with a dire situation. "The train was coming from behind the stock shed. You make a turn, and you're right on top of the tracks."

In 1934, Jim attended another double funeral.

Jim's cousin Cyril Remegus Langer and Mildred Helmenstein had more in common than their marriage. Cyril and Mildred were both of German immigrant heritage; they were raised on rich Wisconsin farmland with many relatives living nearby; and both had lost parents when they were younger than 10.

Yet their extended families were largely different, as were their personalities. This is according to Cyril's biography, preserved by his daughter, Judith Corning of Albany, California. Filling the biography are details gleaned from discussions Cyril had with Judith's husband, Gene, as well as from other snippets of information gathered from relatives, and from Judith's own memories.

The biography seemed to answer a key question—did Cyril work for Lazers Motors in 1927 when his buddy Johnny Pirkl bought a new Chevrolet? From calculating the years in Cyril's early career, it appears not.

Judith wrote a startling detail in a letter. Despite the fact her father stood up as best man in his friend's wedding on the same day his buddy would die, he never told her about it. Yet, having seen that pattern in many other people, it was not surprising to me that he had remained silent about the wedding and the tragedy. Few who lived through the event talked about it. Perhaps, they thought, if they didn't talk about it, it would be less painful; that silence would allow the horrific memories to fade.

"I found out about the Pirkl wedding only in recent years," Judith wrote. "I think it only came to my attention after I got more involved in the Langer family history somehow."

Cyril's grandparents, Edward Langer and Theresa Kunz, married and landed in New York in July 1874, after leaving Rudelsdorf, Austria, with their son Edward. They settled in the Marshall area on a farm, on what became Langer Road, where they raised seven boys and a daughter. Their son Edward married Theresa Frances Nesser, and Ed and Theresa's son Cyril was born on this 70-acre farm.

Jim Langer's parents, Remegius and Amelia Langer, were baptismal sponsors for Cyril, whose middle name also was Remegus, spelled without the "i", his daughter explained. Often, people called Cyril "Mick."

Cyril's parents raised crops and kept cows, and his dad did well as a farmer; he owned his farm and had $1,000 in the bank. But autumn rains triggered a case of pleurisy. Edward continued working, and the pleurisy developed into what was incorrectly diagnosed as tuberculosis.

When Edward was sent to a sanitarium, his brother Emil moved to the farm to help Theresa. She was very worried about her husband and ultimately died of a stroke. "My father always told me his mother died of a broken heart," Judith wrote in the biography.

With their mother dead and their father in the sanitarium, little Cyril and his siblings, Merlin and Valeria, had few options. Their Grandpa Edward lived nearby, but he was in his 60s, had already raised a large family, and was either not able or unwilling to take them in. Besides, he had retired and had given the farm—except for a 10-acre plot on Oak Park Road where he built his retirement home—to his son Charlie. Less than a year earlier, Charlie had married Martha Klecker, my Grandpa Klecker's sister.

Despite her young age, Martha suddenly found herself caretaker to her brother-in-law's three children. And despite Edward's reluctance to take in his grandchildren, Cyril was his favorite, spending enough time with his grandparents to learn the German language.

By the time his father finally left the sanitarium, Cyril had stayed back a year in school because of scarlet fever and whooping cough. Yet when he entered fifth grade, he was so far ahead of his fellow students that he was promoted to sixth grade. Cyril's positive attitude toward school undoubtedly had something to do with his success. He always did well; he especially liked history, and—because he often completed his work early—he'd help other students with their assignments.

Cyril remembered boyhood days of swimming in a hole below the mill-dam in Marshall, while the older boys swam in the river's wider stretch above the dam. Cyril and Merlin also trapped skunks for cash when they were about nine and 10 years old. Cyril loved to tell about the time he got sprayed by a skunk before school and was sent home.

Cyril finished high school in Marshall. He then went to work as a rod-man with an engineering crew and became interested in pursuing an engineering degree. But when he applied at Milwaukee's Marquette University, he learned he was already making more money than engineers who were beginning their careers. He abandoned his plans for college, and, for the next five or six years—except for the winter months—he worked on road crews.

One winter, when Cyril was without a job, an acquaintance who worked at Bill Beneen's Pontiac and Willis auto dealership in Waterloo suggested to Cyril that he apply for employment. He landed a sales position that paid $25 a week, and the job included a car for him to drive. This was "better than sitting around doing nothing." It marked the beginning of his career in the auto industry; a livelihood that would ultimately span six decades.

A few years later, Cyril acquired a contract to sell Pontiacs, and he rented two bays in a repair garage in Deansville. Then he moved to Marshall and sold Chevrolets for Lazers, and he sold Pontiacs for himself, establishing a long relationship with those two automotive brands.

At about that time, Cyril met Milly Helmenstein, one year his senior.

Originally from the Mount Horeb area, she was in the midst of an 11-year stint as a schoolteacher in Marshall. Both were living at the Copeland Hotel. It wasn't until her mom's funeral that Judith Corning heard how her parents met.

"Evidently, Cyril had told the Methodist minister, who officiated at the funeral, that Milly—having heard that Cyril had a real vehicle—ran down the hotel steps to get him to take her for a ride," Judith wrote in the biography. "While Cyril was shy, I guess Milly was not! Cyril always said that he had a lot of girlfriends but never met anyone he wanted to marry except my mother, who was evidently a spirited lass in her late 20s."

The couple dated for years before they wed on the day after Christmas in 1935. Her father, Judith said, didn't like to think back to certain times of his life, such as the scandal of getting Milly pregnant before they wed— he a Catholic; she a Methodist.

A year before their marriage, Cyril had taken over a Chevrolet dealership in Sun Prairie. He kept the Chevrolet line and brought in the Pontiac dealership from Marshall. His business was expanding.

Cyril and Milly's son, George Edward, was born in 1936, and Judith Ann arrived in 1939. When Judith was four years old, the family moved to Vine Street in Sun Prairie, a half block from Cyril's business on East Main and half a block from Sacred Hearts, where the children attended Mass with their father. They also attended Sacred Hearts School through eighth grade.

Judith learned at a young age that a businessman is always busy, but she seemed to relish the lifestyle. She spent much time at the Mobil station, where she'd get her bicycle tires pumped up and read the "funny papers" after Sunday Mass. Cyril rotated wrecker duty with his employees and found himself out in all kinds of weather. His daughter enjoyed riding along with him. When he was home, he often was on call. Judith answered the phone, which rang constantly. Always, it was someone looking for Cyril, Cy, C.R., or Mick.

Cyril thought of tavern visits as a form of advertising. And, as Judith recalled, for two blocks on one side of Sun Prairie's Main Street, practically every other business was a bar. Cyril would visit these, buy rounds of beers for everyone, and stay long enough to get to know the farmers and townsfolk. "Maybe this was a remnant from the old country, where taverns figured prominently in the social life of the towns," Judith wrote in the biography. "Certainly, in some of the bars, the old country card games were in regular play, and, very occasionally, my father went there to play 'Scot'—sheepshead."

Judith also remembered trips back to Deansville. "We went in my childhood years to Deansville for wonderful nickel ice cream cones," she wrote. "He knew the food specialty of every town within, I suppose, 50 miles of Sun Prairie. And he continued to enjoy being his own boss, so that when he was hungry for Limburger cheese, he could drive to Stoughton, or wherever, and get some."

The automobile brought mobility to people, and certainly to the Cyril Langer family. "I think owning his own business gave my father considerable pleasure and was definitely a good choice for him," Judith wrote. "There were, however, drawbacks; the main one probably that he worked far more than a 40-hour week. He was gone many nights because that was when his customers were available. This was also true on weekends."

Cyril helped found the Sun Prairie Chamber of Commerce and remained active in it throughout his career, adding to the other countless evening meetings he attended: Lions Club; the Water and Light Commission, which he served on for many years; and the many activities at Sacred Hearts. After a while, Saturday night card club was added to the schedule. Despite all these commitments, Cyril attended almost every Sun Prairie High School football and basketball game, especially when his son, Ed, was playing. He had season tickets to University of Wisconsin football games and traveled through miserable weather to watch his favorite team, the Green Bay Packers.

Soon after Cyril and Milly were married, they met Lyle and Gracie Cronkite at a restaurant at a time in their lives when both couples were trying to manage active little boys. Cyril and Lyle—who was a pharmacist—became best friends, as did Milly and Gracie, who served as confirmation godmother for Milly's daughter, Judith.

"During this long and busy period of time, our family went on fairly frequent vacations, which made up, to some extent, for the time Cyril had to devote to the business," Judith wrote.

The family enjoyed summer trips to northern Wisconsin or to

Yellowstone or Glacier National Park. And they took many trips to Florida during the winter season when business in the auto industry was slow. During these vacations, Cyril would start one of his "famous" diets, dropping from 220 pounds to perhaps 210. "I don't recall a time when I was growing up that he weighed less than 200 pounds, although I'll bet he'd argue with me on that one," Judith wrote. "He told me that he got fat after he grew up, and he always felt much better than he did when he was skinny."

In her father's biography, Judith reflected on his career. "I think of my father's working life in relation to the automobile; after all, he sold them so early in their history, before we as a nation were really into the auto age. And he stopped selling them when they were still seen as totally positive, before we thought in terms of pollution, and congested cities, and the like—the Golden Age of the automobile, as it were.

"Certainly, when I was growing up, it was quite prestigious to be the daughter of an automobile dealer, especially the daughter of a Chevrolet dealer as Chevies were the fastest-selling automobile in the U.S. for most of the time I lived with my parents and afterward, too."

When Cyril retired in the 1970s, it wasn't a joyous time. "He wasn't very happy about retiring, as can be imagined, seeing how much of his life and effort went into his business. At times, he said he wished he had retired earlier so he could have had an easier time redirecting his life; but mostly, he said he didn't like this retirement business."

Retirement wouldn't find Cyril in pain-free living for long. Soon afterward, on a winter day, he and Milly were in an auto accident on a slippery road near Watertown. Their car was demolished. While Milly got banged up, Cyril narrowly escaped death. He spent many days in a coma, weeks in the hospital, and more weeks at Sun Prairie's Willows Nursing Home, trying to regain mobility. His knee had been badly smashed and never would function well again. Cyril limped for years and was later confined to a wheelchair, a situation he despised.

"Probably more than anything, he loathed giving up driving . . . ," Judith recalled. "He, nonetheless, kept a vehicle until his death; a symbol, I think, of his freedom. And perhaps no better symbol for someone whose era was, indeed, the era of the emergence of the automobile."

Milly died in 1994, and Cyril passed away a few months later, on September 24, at age 90.

The automobile had provided Cyril Langer with a successful career, an easy mode of transportation unimagined by his ancestors, and a life of prominence and stature in the Sun Prairie community. But the auto had, once again, led to tragedy and pain.

After Johnny and Hazel died, Cyril had forged on, with the support of a new friend, Lyle Cronkite. And, in spite of the many drawbacks and disappointments in retirement, the former businessman attempted to shape a pleasant life and exhibit a cheerful disposition until the day he passed on, joining his wife, and Johnny and Hazel on a little hilltop in Marshall known as St. Mary's Catholic Cemetery.

Clan of Cousins

*"The car was sitting there on the grass by the windmill when
we were coming home from school."*

The olfactory experience pulled me back at least 30 years, the
scent of fresh leather enveloping Johnson Shoe Service, Ted
Johnson's shop in Marshall. Tanned strips and slabs of animal
hide filled the place like a vehicle fills a one-car garage—and
the shop was just about that size.

I had known of Ted Johnson's shop from the era when shoes were
expensive; when good ones, made with quality leather, were repaired
instead of being replaced with new ones from the mall. The shop on North
Pardee Street was across the street and very close to the large home my
Grandpa and Grandma Klecker once owned. As a boy, I would travel down
Park Street, loop around the big robin's-egg-blue water tower, and swing
south to get to the shop. I'd take shoes there to have stitching redone, soles
replaced, or to buy a tin of shoe polish or a set of new laces.

Ted would generally tend to my needs. At other times, Charles, his
brother and partner in the shop, was there, and the two worked the leather
side by side. They bought the property in 1956, after it had sat idle for
years. "Charlie went in and fixed several pairs of shoes for his family," Ted
said. "Then the rest of our relatives heard about it and sent us their shoes
that needed fixing. Pretty soon, word spread." The brothers worked the

shop part-time while they held other jobs. Ted finally bought out Charles in 1976.

I got to know Charles first. His youngest son, Barry, was my classmate. Barry lived around the corner from our house. His home faced Firemen's Park, where the water tower stood sentinel above the riverfront. Instead of walking around the corner to Barry's house, it was simpler to cut across the back lots along the power line easement to Johnsons' backyard. Barry and I would spend lazy summer days playing catch and flying kites in the park, or building and painting wooden lawn ornaments—such as squirrels or rabbits—to sell around the neighborhood.

Barry was hardheaded; his two older brothers were tough guys, and that was the only way Barry could survive the brotherly dust-ups. Older bullies, including Joel Olson—who lived next door to Ted Johnson's house—would wait in ambush for Barry and me to come along. They'd push us around or pelt us with snowballs. But Barry wouldn't back down. He'd return snowballs that he'd take pains to make firm in his leather mittens, to the point of being icy.

I dreaded those days. But then, my sister, Karen, who was three years ahead of us in school, befriended her classmate Jim Olson. Jim was Joel's older brother, and soon, Jim took me under his wing. I got to know Joel, and that was the end of the bullying.

Jim became my coach, my mentor, and my friend. I didn't know anything about sports before he came into my life. We'd practice baseball, football, and basketball. Jim encouraged me to read the sports section of the newspaper to keep up with our favorite teams. When I think back on that, it probably led to my interest in a journalism profession that has spanned more than a quarter century—nearly as long as it has been since I last saw Jim.

Jim became my Little League baseball coach. There were four teams— the Braves, Cubs, Reds, and White Sox. We were the Cubs, despite our green shirts. I played shortstop. But my baseball career ended suddenly. I was clowning around with a kid's banana-seat bike on our next-door neighbor's front lawn. I tried doing a wheelie and pulled up too hard, and the bike flipped backwards. I reached out with my left arm, elbow locked to brace my fall. The elbow snapped. The cast came off the day of the Little League's season-ending party at Firemen's Park.

In my shortened season, I went 1-for-9 at the plate, my only base hit coming against White Sox pitcher Barry Johnson. I never again played organized baseball.

Barry and I played a lot of basketball in his driveway, too, but he was more of a football player. He was somewhat stiff-jointed, and when someone in school learned he couldn't sit "Indian" style, he was dubbed "Stiff"—a nickname that followed him through his school days.

Barry and I made the varsity basketball team, but back in seventh grade we heard a memorable comment. Claus Lindquist, our junior high school physical education teacher and seventh-grade basketball coach, was from Finland. He knew skiing and soccer, but he had never seen the game of basketball played until he arrived in Marshall for a one-year coaching stint. While we didn't appreciate his lack of basketball knowledge, we did enjoy his accent, which brought us a huge laugh when Barry tossed up another errant outside shot during a practice.

"Jonesewn, vat you shootin' for now? You know you caun't make it!" the coach bellowed in his funny accent, as we roared in laughter. We never let Barry forget that comment.

Barry's parents both died of cancer around 1980, oddly, within six months of each other. So I visited Ted in the hope of gaining insight into the Pirkl family. The Johnsons grew up on a farm at the end of Langer Road, near the Pirkl farm. Stan Johnson still worked the Johnson place.

Ted was born in 1928, nearly a year after the deaths of Johnny Pirkl and his new bride. He knew Johnny's brother, Frank, and he shared another fact about the two families that startled me. They were related. Ted Johnson's parents were John and Evelyn. John's mother was the former Mary Hady, a sister to Johnny Pirkl's mother, the former Barbara Hady. That made Johnny Pirkl a first cousin of Ted's father, John Johnson.

John Johnson was born in 1896, and in 1920 he wed 17-year-old Evelyn Chadwick. The couple raised seven boys and two girls on the farm overlooking the Pirkl place. Ted was able to provide all the birth dates as well as the dates of death. Delbert, or Adelbert, was born in 1921. He told me Delbert suffered from Alzheimer's disease and was in a local nursing home. Lawrence was born in 1922, Charles in 1924. Then came Harold—

or was it Sterling?—in 1926. Someone erred on his birth certificate, Ted explained.

"He thought his name was Sterling, but he went into the service and found out he got 'Harold Sterling' instead of 'Sterling Harold.' Instead of changing his birth certificate, he changed his name. Sometimes, we'd get mail and wonder who it was for."

Stanley was born in 1927, the same year Johnny Pirkl died. Then came Ted; then Willard, who died in 1993. When he got to Willard, I reminded Ted that I asked him to give me the birth dates in order; not boys first, followed by girls. That's what he did! "Dad wasn't going to quit until he had some girls."

Finally, Evelyn arrived in 1932. Janice was born two years later.

Ted leaned over the little counter, taking time to tell stories, squinting behind his glasses as he'd chuckle about an incident, and rubbing one hand with the other to ward off numbness from an old injury. Two signs hung above his head. One read: Smoking not allowed. The other one: When all is said and done, more will be said than done.

Ted's father always attended St. Mary's Catholic Church; in fact, a 1926-28 financial statement for St. Mary's lists J.A. Johnson as giving 10 dollars each year. He and Evelyn were married at St Mary's, Father C.M. Nellen officiating, but she always attended the United Methodist Church. Their children were raised Methodist, an arrangement that, as Ted noted, was unusual for that time.

One day in 1998, I stopped at my mother's house for lunch, and when I told her I had met Janice Johnson, she told me that Janice was one of my father's old girlfriends. Mom continued to elaborate, but I chose to ignore her words.

I visited Janice because Ted said she would have documents detailing the family's history. She married Vernon Weihert. They lived close to Portland, a burg just northeast of Waterloo on Highway 19.

Between Janice and Ted, I pieced together scraps of information on Johnson farm life. The family raised dairy cattle and 30 pigs or so with two or three sows. After they did away with the sows, they'd buy between 30 and 60 feeder pigs at the Watertown fair and fatten them up. In the 1940s, they gave up raising pigs.

The Johnson family used a bobsled in winter to transport milk cans to the creamery. "We'd leave the car at the top of the hill and walk down the driveway to the house if it was snowy or muddy," Janice said. "I can remember the snowbanks as high as the apple trees some winters. You don't have snowstorms like that around here anymore."

The marshy area of the Johnson farm was often too wet to work, even after it was dredged, Ted said. It did, however, make good pheasant and rabbit habitat among the tamaracks and hardwoods, a fine spot for Ted to hone his hunting skills. Because of the lowlands, John Johnson bought another 120-acre farm near the intersection of County T and Langer Road. "We needed the high land for oats and alfalfa," Ted said. "At the home place, only about 40 acres were on high land."

Vincent Johnson was born in Cerna, Bohemia, Austria, in 1848, according to an obituary I borrowed from Janice. At age 18, he came to America with his parents, brothers, and sisters and settled in Watertown. He married Mary Hady in Watertown in the early 1870s, arriving at the farm southwest of Marshall in 1877. Eventually the couple had a dozen children. "He was a good husband and father, a congenial friend and neighbor and will be greatly missed by all who knew him," his 1917 obituary reads.

Mary Hady's early life was remarkably similar to her future husband's. Born in Austria in 1853, she arrived in America with her family in 1868 and settled in Watertown. When Mary Hady Johnson died in 1939 at age 86, the list of survivors included 22 grandchildren, eight great-grandchildren, a sister, Barbara Pirkl of Marshall, and a brother, Michael Hady of Pine City, Minnesota.

"Mrs. Johnson has lived an active, useful life, filled with love and care for her family and dear ones," her obituary read. "She had been ill for several weeks, but her condition had so improved that her sudden death on Saturday was a shock to the family and friends." She was a "faithful" member of St. Mary's Catholic Church in Marshall, her obituary stated. Services for Mary and Vincent were both at St. Mary's, and both lie buried in the church cemetery.

Janice Johnson showed me a photo of one of the children who survived the parents. It was of her father, John A. Johnson. "My dad was not a real big man," Janice said. "He was a nice man." The photo showed a trim, although stout-looking man with a wide, prominent forehead.

"Mom was always in the kitchen, baking bread every other day. She was always cooking," Janice said, and with Evelyn's brood of nine, one could understand why. Amazingly, Evelyn found time for music. "She played the piano whenever she had time. She could play everything. She'd play for plays, the opera house, silent movies—whatever shows were in town."

"Yo."

That's how Lawrence Johnson greeted me as his head popped out of the basement stairwell outside his home at the LEJ Ranch on Highway 73, about a half mile south of Marshall.

His siblings had warned me that he was hard of hearing. Despite that impairment, I found him delightfully sharp of wit. I stopped to visit him the same day I'd met with Ted and Janice. Lawrence, being older, might have more memories of the early days of the Johnsons and Pirkls, his siblings suggested. After I explained my reason for stopping, Lawrence, wearing coveralls, set aside his broom and was happy to talk in the frigid, outside air. I suggested we might be more comfortable chatting indoors. Lawrence led me inside and promptly told his wife, Eleanor, that I was an insurance salesman who wanted to talk. Eleanor let out a sarcastic cluck before Lawrence shared my real purpose.

We weren't long into our visit when Lawrence told me he remembered the day in 1927 when the Peck farmhouse burned. He was not yet five years old. "Dad went to help carry water to the fire," he recalled. "I saw the smoke coming up something furious."

Lawrence and I sat at the dining room table, Lawrence reflecting on how his life overlapped the lives of the Pirkls. His wife sat on a chair in the corner, over his left shoulder, helping Lawrence better understand my questions. "Yo," he'd proclaim, whenever he suddenly grasped what I'd asked, or whenever a query jogged his memory.

His family worked the fields with a gasoline-powered 1926 Fordson—an iron-wheeled greenish-gray tractor; the kind that came with a plow and disc, and for which old horse-drawn equipment could be converted. The Johnsons' neighbor beyond the Pirkl farm, Bob Pautsch, also owned one.

"Lots of people had them," he said. In fact, of the farmers who could afford luxuries in the 1920s, perhaps 75 percent owned Fordsons, but not the Pirkls. The Johnsons had double wheels on the back of their Fordson to keep it from sinking in the marsh.

"We'd raise tobacco, leaves as big as a man's torso," Lawrence said. They'd sell the tobacco for the tidy sum of two cents per pound.

Lawrence recalled how Johnny and Frank Pirkl cut the trees off the whole hillside, following their father's instructions. "Joe engineered it so they'd get an extra hour of sunlight on that three-corner piece," Lawrence said, referring to the slice of the former Pirkl land that County T dissects. "When Joe moved to town, he was always hauling wood for his furnace."

Lawrence worked as the hired hand for the neighborhood. He helped at the Pautsch farm when Bob broke his leg. And he often worked for Frank Pirkl when Helen's brother, Alfred Holzman, lived with them. "Frank would call me up and ask me to come help him saw off some trees with the rubbing saw. We'd butcher a pig and hang it up. Frank's was a good place for dinner, that's for sure," said Lawrence, generating sarcastic feedback from the woman seated behind him. "The meat was tender. Helen was German; she could talk German. That's why the meat was so tender—it was German style."

Lawrence remembered the purebred Durham cattle the Pirkls raised— dark red and white ones. Black and blue ones, apparently crossbreeds, were only incidental. "You had to go over the hill to the Pautsch farm to see Guernseys," he said.

Frank's father, Joseph, was around, too. "Joe would come out and hoe in the garden or work in the shop. He had quite a good-looking shop—a blacksmith shop and forge in there. If you needed an axe handle, he'd make one, not go to town."

Janice Weihert and Ted Johnson remembered pieces of information about the Pirkls, too.

Frank Pirkl was on the crew working the threshing machine that Benny Taves owned, Janice said. "Frank was big, broad. He always seemed like a happy person, laughing, and joking."

"Frankie was a fun guy," Ted said. "He was always good for a laugh. He'd always tell polite jokes—he always had the girls there," Ted said of

Frank's daughters, Marian and Joann. "He could tell them in front of the girls."

Janice and Ted's father, John Johnson, served on the Pyburn School Board with Frank Pirkl and Frank's brother-in-law, Ed Walker. "They'd talk about everything besides just school—all being farmers," Janice reflected. "They'd talk until the wee hours of the morning. For the Christmas program, Frank Pirkl would build a stage out of boards; a platform. I don't know how it got to be his job, but he was the one who did that."

Despite the fact that they were related to the Pirkls, not all the Johnsons recalled that Barbara Pirkl and their paternal grandmother were sisters; that Ted, Janice, Lawrence, and their siblings were cousins once-removed to Johnny Pirkl. The relationship even surprised my father. But when I told him, he remembered how the Johnson and Pirkl kids used to refer to each other as cousins.

Lawrence Johnson finished grade school in 1935. "We had to go to Madison West High to get our diplomas," he said. "We got ice cream cones as little tokens."

Lawrence and Eleanor—sister to former Marshall postmaster and historian Stan Trachte—married in 1943. They lived in Madison for two years while Lawrence delivered ice for Oscar Mayer in the summers. He then worked in Sun Prairie for Oconomowoc Canning. "I started during the sweet corn season—just thought I'd work until the season was over. Then they asked me to stay and help out with some winter things. The next thing you know, 39 years have passed," he said, pointing to a retirement plaque on the wall.

The next month would mark the 40th year that Lawrence and Eleanor had lived on the crest of a hill south of Marshall. He raised pigs and red Hereford steers; working full time for the canning company obviously left little time for a dairy herd. Lawrence and his "girl" also raised chickens, geese, and three daughters—Patricia, Sandra, and Beverly.

"Of course, my girl didn't have much to do but count the money," Lawrence quipped.

"That didn't take long," Eleanor fired back with equal wit.

My buddy Mike Taylor remembered Lawrence Johnson well. But it never occurred to me that the Taylor farm, with its buildings on the west side of Oak Park Road, had 20 acres on the east side that butted up to the Lawrence Johnson property. A ditch ran between the farms, Mike explained. Lawrence often planted sweet corn, and he would be sure to tuck eight or 10 rows along the ditch so the big Taylor family could get its fill come picking time.

In his younger days, Mike was among the Taylor siblings who'd help out on Lawrence's farm, often riding over on their 50cc Honda motorcycle. He would shovel manure or do whatever was needed. Lawrence kept a wad of bills rolled up in the chest pocket of his coveralls, and he'd debate and contemplate, in drawn-out fashion, about how much to pay his little farmhands. He always paid well, no matter what the amount, Mike remembered.

In his teen years, Mike worked at Wisconsin Porcelain, a plant in Sun Prairie that stood beside Oconomowoc Canning. Sometimes, Mike would hitch rides to work with Lawrence.

Mike recalled a big snowstorm when the porcelain plant's foremen advised employees not to travel, to work double shifts, or to find a place to sack out. But Lawrence, at the canning company, would have none of that talk. He had farm chores awaitin', after all. Lawrence headed out with his vehicle but got stuck in a snowdrift shortly after leaving Sun Prairie. He hoofed it the rest of the way home.

Ted, Lawrence, and Janice remembered those long walks to Pyburn School. Older people like to weave stories about trudging miles through all kinds of weather to get to school in the days before automobiles. For the Johnson kids, that task was often a daily reality.

Just the thought made me weary as I imagined the options—either follow Langer Road all the way to County T, then head west to the school, or take the shortcut across the Pirkl and Pautsch farms—much shorter but with the hazards of snow, mud, and the steep ridge to the west. It took about 20 minutes in good weather. And if you got cold, as the wind whipped in your face while you trudged across the Pirkl place, you'd certainly be warm by the time you climbed to the top of the ridge.

"When the weather was nice, we'd walk along the cow lane," Ted reflected. "We had a path worn down after a little bit. If it was snowy or muddy, we'd have to walk up to the Yelk farm and then follow the line fence. Sometimes, we'd get two feet of water in the marsh in the spring.

"We'd always end up in Frankie's dooryard, except when it was real nice. If Frankie wasn't real busy, we'd crowd into his Ford and go to school. Frankie had a hired hand, and he figured he could take off a little easier. If we arrived early and he was doing something, he'd ask us to wait. If it was raining, he'd always take us. There was a bunch of us—four or five Johnsons. When one would graduate, another would start."

Ted remembered rides in Frank's four-door Ford, a 1938 or 1939. But he also recalled rides, when he was seven years old, maybe nine, in Johnny's 1927 Chevy. "We also got rides home from school when it was raining if Joe Pirkl was out working at the farm. It ran good," Ted said of the Chevy with the tragic past. "We had an old '28, so we were used to riding in the box cars."

Besides nasty weather, Ted remembered another reason why his siblings and the Pirkl girls couldn't always walk over the hill to school. "If the Pirkls had a boar up in the woods, we couldn't cut through there on the way to school."

Janice recalled a tactic little Joann Pirkl used to convince her father they needed a lift to school. "If Joann would cry a little, he'd give us all a ride," Janice said.

Later reminded of that tactic, Joann responded: "They had me trained pretty well."

"We were a little more spoiled than the Johnson kids," Joann's sister, Marian, added. "I don't think Johnny Johnson ever drove his kids to school."

Janice also tormented Joann with a dead snake if they came upon one on the gravel road. "Oh, I'd scream and run," Joann said.

If the Johnsons and Pirkls ended up walking across the Pautsch farm, the trip could prove to be both tasty and unpleasant. "We'd pick apples off the ground to eat from the orchard at the Pautsch farm," Janice reflected, "and Mrs. Pautsch would come out and shake a finger at us. The Pautsches had a dog. We were scared to death of that dog."

My father often walked along with the Johnson and Pirkl clans on the way to school. Dad also recalled those rainy-day rides to school, and how

Frank would stop his '41 Ford to give him a ride, too, if the car wasn't already loaded with kids.

One day, however, it was raining and Frank's car was full. Still, he stopped, and Dad and another neighbor sat on the back bumper, bouncing their feet along the road to keep from falling off because the car's straight rear end afforded no room to lean back for balance. Such an unsafe arrangement would cause a public outcry these days; in those days, it was nothing more than a school board member helping a couple of kids get to classes on a rainy day.

"We saw them frequently with the car," Lawrence said of the Pirkls, with Joe behind the wheel of Johnny's 1927 Chevy.

While he was on the subject of cars, Lawrence told me his family bought a 1928 Chevy for $700. Meanwhile, Frank Pirkl bought a 1928 Model A Ford. "We took it out on Highway 19 and goosed it up that hill," he said of the steep hill a mile or so west of Marshall. "Frank said he'd get it going 60; if you could get up that hill without losing zip, you had a good machine."

He added: "When you'd buy a car from Frank Lazers, you'd get a free kite, a Red Crown Sky Skimmer, with the red crown gasoline emblem on it."

I wondered if the playful Johnny Pirkl ever flew such a kite.

Catherine Benesch, left, and her mother, Edie. Right: The children of Edie Pirkl and Edward Benesch, c. 1926, at the Benesch farm on Marshall's north side: Leo, standing, Catherine, and baby Jim.

Jim Benesch poses in the home his grandparents, Joseph and Barbara Pirkl, once owned in Marshall. The home was the scene of a wedding party for Johnny and Hazel Pirkl, and days later their wake.

Family Ties

"Oh, God, I hit that car!"

Jim Benesch was born December 30, 1925, making him less than two years old when his Uncle Johnny died, so he had no memory of Johnny. But he remembered that day of the bicycle race like it was yesterday.

Jim recalled a time when he and his buddy Charlie Skala were freshmen in high school. They were returning to school after their lunch break, and their bike ride took them past Jim's Grandpa and Grandma Pirkl's house. "I had a beautiful bicycle with balloon tires. It was fancy. It had a horn and headlight; everybody wanted to ride my bike. I had front brake drums on it."

Charlie and Jim decided to race back to school. "We were pedaling as fast as we could," Jim recalled, between puffs of cigarettes. "I got to the corner in front of Grandma's, and I whipped up on the sidewalk. Grandma was watching through the window."

Grandma Pirkl, busy at the kitchen sink, glanced out and saw danger unfold before her eyes. It happened so quickly, she could do little but yell in futility. Grandpa Pirkl, you see, was backing Johnny's car out of the garage.

"I looked back to see where Charlie was and WHAM! The next thing I knew, I was half on the running board, and half on the ground, looking up at Grandpa, who was looking down at me through the car window. Grandma had been hollering out the window, 'Jimmy! Look out!' She almost fainted. Oh, God, I hit that car!"

The impact dented the side of the car, but the way autos were built in those days, "You could just hit it, and it would pop back out," Jim said. However, the wheel and fork of his fancy bike were bent. Only Jim's pride was hurt. "Grandpa never chewed me out or anything. I was surprised. We laughed about it later. 'Gees, you musta really been coming.'"

In March of 1998, I was visiting with Jim and Ormae Benesch in the attractive mobile home they had occupied for several decades. It's one of many in a vast spread called Evergreen Park on Marshall's west side. Across the street, geese and ducks were floating on the pond and in the channel that splits the park. The fowl were everywhere, waddling out of the way of cars; soiling the Benesch lawn and driveway. A hundred or more mobile homes, including the Benesches', spread out north of the channel, and per-haps another hundred stretch beyond the combination clubhouse-office building to the south.

I think back to my teen years when my buddies and I worked for Evergreen Park. Cyril Motl—whose daughter Judy married my Uncle Fran Klecker—developed Evergreen Park. I grew up thinking Cyril basi-cally owned Marshall. And maybe that assumption wasn't so far off. Cyril developed a strip of shops close to Evergreen Park. At one time, Uncle Fran and Aunt Judy managed a restaurant, Park Place, that was nestled among a group of shops and eventually became known as the Cobblestone.

I was hired as a dishwasher at Park Place. But I hated it; I dreaded the heat, sweat, and too many dirty dishes coming at me too fast. I had the crummy shifts: Friday and Saturday nights, and Tuesdays—the night of the kitchen's weekly scrub-down. After my first night, I vowed to find another job. But I stuck it out for a while, learning to have fun with my co-work-ers. I especially enjoyed it when Kendra Langer, daughter of my grade school principal, wore that cute, short, black and white waitress outfit and bent over to get sweet rolls from the heated drawer behind the power dish-washer.

I worked at Park Place for the better part of a year. Later, Fran and Judy became managers at Evergreen Park, so I got a job there. The employees enjoyed crazy times at the work shed, where the park equipment was stored. That's where Karl Loewen taught me how to start an old Jeep by pushing it and popping the clutch; where we'd blow up soda cans with M-80s; and where we'd build storage sheds for the mobile homes between telling jokes and goofing off.

The other guys thought it was great fun to run around with the big riding mowers. I wasn't much into that. Maybe I'd mowed too many lawns in my younger days, riding the 12-horse Massey-Ferguson to and from the Peck farm and to a vacant lot along the muddy Maunesha. That was how I had earned my pocket cash. Now, I favored building the sheds, even if it meant working alone while the others mowed. Building a shed "solo" was no small feat because I had to support part of the structure with one hand and juggle both the screw and screwdriver with the other. I challenged myself to see how fast I could assemble an entire 10-foot-by-10-foot shed. Top speed was about four hours, as I recall.

But now, Jim Benesch was the one doing the recalling. And the memories flowed as fast as he went from one cigarette to the next. At least a ceiling fan was sucking out the smoky stench, and the mobile home didn't seem as suffocating as I remembered it from an earlier time.

That's right. I'd been here before. You see, when I started talking to people about Johnny and Hazel Pirkl, I had no idea that Jim was Johnny's nephew. All I knew was that Jim and Ormae were the parents of an only child, Steve—a big, bearded, bespectacled math and computer whiz who happened to marry my sister, Karen, in 1972.

I always enjoyed Jim Benesch, despite his cigarettes. I enjoyed the way he welcomed me when I'd stop to visit; his girlie magazines; his laugh. And now, he occasionally broke into that infectious chuckle as he recalled his grandparents and his boyhood days on the Benesch farm along Highway 73 on Marshall's north edge.

In 1913, when Edward Benesch married Edith Pirkl, her brother Johnny was 11. Ed and Edith raised three children on that farm off Highway 73. Catherine was born in 1916; Leo was born in 1918; and Jim came along more than seven years later. "I was an accident, I guess," Jim said with a laugh.

Jim's Grandpa Vincent and his family lived in a log cabin when they came to Marshall. The cabin stood beyond a pond to the north of Canal Road, just west of the wooded land where Vincent Benesch later would drive his team of horses, build a barn and farmhouse, and carve farm fields. "My dad and I walked back there to the cabin site when I was a kid," Jim said. "Back then, there were just a few stones and apple trees there."

At the farm, Vincent and his wife, the former Catherine Hamshire, raised six kids. Edward was born April 15, 1890.

Vincent Benesch raised navy beans, his first crop. "You'd flail 'em out on the plank floor of the old barn," Jim recalled.

Son Edward later raised hogs and milked Brown Swiss on the same farm. "Dad had a nice herd of cattle," Jim said. "He was fussy with his cattle and his horses."

Topsy and Dan were Ed Benesch's prized Percherons. "That one team of horses, I don't think you could have bought for any price," Jim said with a distant look, as if he still could see their rippling muscles pulling a plow through stubborn soil. "You didn't need any lines to lead them. Whatever you told them to do, that's what they did, whether they were hooked to a bobsled, a hay wagon, or a cultivator. When cultivating, you'd just turn them again, and they knew which row to take next. When Ma rang the dinner bell, they'd get to the end of the row, and they'd turn and go down the field road. They knew it was time for dinner.

"If somebody got stuck in the field, you'd unhook their team and hook up Topsy and Dan to pull 'em out. They'd get their feet set just right, and it was going to come out. They'd just lean into it. I never saw a team pull like that. If someone's manure spreader was mired in the mud to the axle with a load of shit on it, it was never mired with that team. They'd drag that sucker until it killed them. They worked together. Topsy was a little smaller, but they pulled right together with each other. They were gentle, too. You could crawl under them and hook the harnesses on."

Still, technology finally caught up with the aging workhorses. "When we got a 1942 Model A John Deere, the ground was so hard that year you couldn't get the horse cultivator in the ground," Jim said. "Dad sold Topsy and Dan for $500 when you couldn't get $100 for a team anymore. Pa had to get rid of them; he hardly used them anymore. We had another team, and Topsy and Dan were getting up in age. Dad couldn't turn down $500."

Topsy and Dan weren't the only quality work animals on the farm. "We had a dog named Tippy, an English shepherd. We'd have cattle, hogs, and horses out in the woods pasture. You'd tell Tippy to go get whichever, and he'd bring the right ones back. We'd go in for supper, and by the time we got done, he'd have the cows in the lane, ready to come in for milking. He'd nip at the backs of the hooves, and the cows would kick, and he'd flatten out, and the hoof would go right over his head. Tippy was like another person on the farm. No money could buy a dog like that."

Tippy was mostly white and tan with a gray saddle across his back. "In the summer, Pa would clip his coat and leave a tuft of hair on the end of his tail. Tippy would wag it, and look back at it, and act cocky."

Ed Benesch was fond of his animals, and he was fond of hog farming. "When the sows were farrowing, Dad would be out in the barn with the sows in 20-below-zero weather. He'd come rushing in with a bushel basket full of piglets and open the oven door and let them get warm. Then he'd take them back out to suckle."

The family raised about 200 chickens and kept a few sheep for the kids' Future Farmers of America projects. The pigs would eat acorns in the woods where Highway 73 now makes a sharp turn to the right. Sometimes the animals wouldn't return to feed in the yard for a few days.

Jim's dad planted sweet clover and plowed it under in the spring for a natural fertilizer. "It made nice, loose ground. When Dad would walk behind the team of horses, he'd find arrowheads."

Meanwhile, Jim's mother was busy cleaning and cooking. "When Mom did the wash depended on which way the wind was blowing the dust from the gravel off Highway 73.

"Mother was a helluva good cook and baker. We never had trouble keeping hired men—the food was always good. They'd get paid $25 or $30 per month during the Depression—those were good wages. Mom did her canning and baking on a wood range. We never bought a loaf of bread."

Jim's mother bought a new black walnut table—one with about 10 extension leaves—from Sorenson's Furniture Store. It was delivered just in time for a threshing party. "She got all the stuff on it, and it broke right in half, and all the stuff slid together. That was a helluva performance. Mom called Sorensons, and they brought a different one right out."

Life on the farm was hard, but it wasn't without good times. Jim's parents were strict, but not overly so. "I never got a licking. When they said something, you did it."

Jim recalled when his brother, Leo, pitched for Lazers' city baseball team in Marshall. "He pitched a no-hitter once, but he screwed up his arm and had to quit pitching. We had a diamond in the lower cow pasture at our farm. We had games there on Sundays. We had a Brown Swiss bull that kept bellowing when the cars rolled in for the Sunday games. He didn't like those cars on that gravel driveway down by the barn. He wouldn't quit bellowing until he was damn good and ready."

When Jim's parents celebrated their 25th wedding anniversary in 1938, they rolled up the carpet and guests danced to accordion music. Friends and relatives enjoyed home brew, apple cider, and popcorn. Kerosene lamps illuminated boisterous card games. "Someone would hit the table so hard while playing cards that the chimney on the lamp would pop off. You'd have to juggle the hot thing to put it back on."

The Benesch farm had no electricity for decades. "One time, when I was a kid, someone opened the door, and the wind blew the kerosene lamp out," Jim said. "I ran over to help get it relighted and grabbed the chimney. My hide and fingerprints were on that damn globe." His mother used butter to salve Jim's wounds.

When the wonder of electrical power finally arrived, Ed Benesch bought poles and wires. "I was in seventh or eighth grade," Jim said. "Bakers lived across the road from us; they got lights at the same time. We each turned on all our lights and stood out on Highway 73 and looked out over the lights."

I knew Leo Benesch and his wife, Doris, who continued to farm the Benesch homestead. I remembered Leo as a jolly guy with a physique to match his nature. And I'd been to their farm more than once. I spent several weeks helping Roelof Kraak with a roofing and remodeling project on the farmhouse where Leo, Jim, and Catherine Benesch grew up. For almost two years while I was in high school, and beyond, I spent summers and other breaks helping Kraak build houses.

It was summertime when we worked at the Benesch farm—a comfortable place to be when Leo's youngest daughter, Wendy, was out and about. Wendy was obviously too distracting because she pointed out my indiscretions in my senior yearbook: "What can I say to someone who stared at me all summer while I mowed lawn?"

Mitsy, as she was known, was a year behind me in school and much more fond of a guy named—no kidding—Newton Newton. He was named after his paternal grandfather, whose first name was Newton. Newton also was the maiden name of Newton's mother. When his parents died young, his mother's brother adopted him—thus the name Newton Newton.

Newton was a curly haired, chunky guy whose name was as funny as his demeanor. I knew him well in our younger years. Countless times we battled each other, one-on-one, on my driveway basketball court, and I was his substitute on his newspaper route. Sadly, Newton died in 1998, the weekend of the annual Firemen's Festival in Marshall, at age 41. Survivors included two sons and his wife, Wendy.

Jim Benesch married the former Ormae Schafer in 1947. Jim got a job grading highways in the town of Medina but left because the grader kept breaking down. He and Ormae bought a mobile home, and Jim went to work for Creamery Package in Lake Mills. But when Jim was laid off, he and Ormae pulled their mobile home onto the Benesch homestead, and Jim farmed with his brother for a spell. Jim moved from job to job nearly as often as a farmer rotates his crops.

"My big fear was that I was going to be without a job sometime," he recalled. Among his many jobs, he worked in maintenance at Marshall's schools for more than 13 years; a stint during which a skinny grade-schooler named Greg Peck first became familiar with one Jim Benesch.

No matter what job he had at the time, Jim Benesch remained close to his mother, who died in 1983. She outlived her husband, Ed, by more than three decades. "Mom was a wonderful person, always just so," Jim said. "She never got real mad. A hard worker. She'd help milk the cows by hand. She suffered many years with arthritis but never complained about it."

In her latter years, Jim would call and ask how her arthritis was. "'Oh, pretty good,' she'd say. Then I'd see her a couple of days later and ask her the same question, and she'd say, 'Oh, a couple of days ago, I was really hurting.' But she'd never admit it when I was over there. She was so sweet."

Edith Benesch played the piano and organ at St. Mary's Church, despite her crippling arthritis. Jim recalled that his Aunt Altie Walker wound up with his mother's organ, and the piano went to the Pirkl house in town. "It was upright, open. The easiest-playing piano; you just touch those keys. A beautiful-sounding piano."

The piano ended up with a tenant who was living downtown above Kleinsteiber's store. Jim, his Uncle Frank Pirkl, and about a half-dozen other fellas muscled the music machine up the creaky outside steps. It wasn't until afterward that they realized just how perilous the task was. "You wouldn't have hauled two five-gallon pails of shit up those steps, they were so rotted."

Later, when it was time to remove the old piano, the owners busted it up to get it down the stairs.

Jim lit another cigarette. Maybe his love for tobacco was hereditary. His dad chewed PlowBoy tobacco and smoked it in a pipe. Ed Benesch also smoked cigars. He favored Phillies. Jim's grandfather, Joe Pirkl, enjoyed tobacco, too, raising a few plants to satisfy his needs.

"He always had homespun—that's what he called it—tobacco that he used in his pipe. He smoked Harvester cigars, too. I used to get the cigar bands from him. I had a cigar band collection at one time. He'd smoke cigars with Uncle Leonard and Frankie on Sundays and during get-togethers."

Jim's sister threw away his little collection. But it didn't prevent him from a lifelong tobacco habit, carrying the torch for tobacco like his father and his uncles before him, and like his Grandpa Joe. Whatever health concerns tobacco creates, the stuff had done nothing to diminish Jim Benesch's memory.

"Grandpa Joe was a tall man, always walked pretty straight. He was very stern. If we were visiting and us kids got to making too much noise, he'd let us know right now."

Jim remembered when members of St. Mary's congregation met to discuss the matter of putting a fence around the Catholic cemetery. "Grandpa wasn't much for it, but he let 'em argue awhile. Then he got up and said there wasn't anybody wants to get in there very bad and the ones that are in there don't want to get out. That's all he said, and that ended that argument."

To this day, no fence surrounds St. Mary's Cemetery.

Jim Benesch has fond memories of his Grandma Barbara Pirkl, too. "Grandma Pirkl was everybody's grandma that went to school," Jim recalled. "If they were sick to their stomach, or the girls got their first period, or someone got bruised or scratched, she fixed 'em up."

For upset stomachs, Grandma Pirkl used chamomile, a bitter flower blossom that looks like little daisies with white petals and yellow centers. "She always had a jar with big white peppermint candies, about as big as a nickel, for us. She was a wonderful person. She'd do anything for anybody."

Jim seemed to recall that his Grandma Barbara lived for a while on the Johnson farm overlooking the Pirkl place. After all, Vincent Johnson's wife, Mary, was a sister to the former Barbara Hady. When a young Joe Pirkl came courting, Grandma Barbara told Jim, she used to say, "Here comes the beanpole."

"Grandpa liked to tell a story of Grandma's dream. She was milking cows and saw a cat sitting on the edge of a milk bucket. She was going to kick the cat out of there, and she kicked the wall in her sleep and broke her big toe. He thought that was funny."

Jim chuckled over another story. "One time, Grandma Pirkl was going to make a custard pie for Grandpa. It must have had a hole in it because all the custard sank to the bottom and the crust was on the top when she took it out of the oven. All it took was one pinhole, I guess. Pa and Grandma used to laugh about that one.

"Grandma, like my mother, never fretted about anything. She always thought some good came out of anything. A fellow . . . shot his girlfriend. Mom said, 'We'll never know the suffering that woman might have had.' That was their attitude. Nothing could happen so bad that some good couldn't come out of it. They always found a bright side, possibly, to most anything."

Grandma Pirkl may not have fretted, but she ate a lot of garlic because it was supposed to be good for the heart. But for Barbara Pirkl, matriarch of the family, the woman who'd witnessed so much sorrow, who buried two of her seven children, the end came on November 11, 1950, a month shy of her 85th birthday.

"Grandma died going to the dentist, Dr. Joyce, in Waterloo," Jim recalled. The dentist's office was in the upstairs of a big home downtown. "It was a hellish long stairs. She got up to the top and dropped over dead," Jim said, although her obituary listed St. Mary's Hospital in Columbus as the spot where she was pronounced dead after being transported there.

"It didn't pay for her to go get her teeth fixed, I guess."

Jim recalled the brutal nature of early dentistry. "He'd pull a tooth by putting his knee on your chest," Jim said of Dr. Joyce. "He even broke some jaws."

Jim's cousin, Marian Zimbric, later told me that her Grandma Pirkl had been on her way to have a tooth pulled. Maybe it wasn't the long stairway that killed Barbara Pirkl, but the fear.

Jim recalled much about his grandparents' home in Marshall, the one where Johnny and his new bride were laid out in their wedding attire, pale faces at rest in wooden coffins.

Jim, too, was looking rather pale, much older, in February 1999, a few months after his wife, Ormae, succumbed to a horrible struggle with cancer. Grief had become his constant companion. I couldn't seem to reach him on his portable phone, so I stopped in to see if he had time to revisit his grandparents' former home.

Jim sat in the smoky mobile home, the TV blaring on the Game Show Network. He couldn't go that day, he said; he was doing laundry. When I suggested the next day, he agreed, hesitantly. I stayed awhile, asked a few more questions, and showed him some old family photos that I had acquired.

When I picked him up the next day, he wore the same shirt; a yellow stain still in the collar area. He was drinking a cup of milk and eating unpalatable looking sliced meat he'd bought at the meat market, something with cheese chunks in it. He told me what it was, but I couldn't hear him over the TV; I dared not ask again, lest he'd think I was interested in sampling it. Lunch finished, he went into the bedroom or the bathroom for a minute and returned on weak, shaky legs. He wore the same shirt.

"No sense changing my shirt, they're not that fancy over there," he said. I was thankful he zipped up his coat and covered his shirt.

Outside, he took a few puffs on a fresh cigarette, and then he put it out, without my need to ask that of him, before he climbed into my truck. We headed to 227 Porter Street to meet with Ruth Lochner who, along with her husband, Mike, owned the former Joseph Pirkl home.

Walter Hamshire, who had lived across the street from St. Mary's Church for decades, had told me it was quite a thing when Joe Pirkl built the house. "There wasn't too much building back then," Walter said. "When someone's building a new house, that was news. You went and looked at it. Probably none were built again until 10 years later; that was just before the Depression."

Jim and I took the snowy, icy path up to the front door, crossing the porch that spanned the front of the house, and we entered the dining room in a spot where Grandpa Pirkl once sat in his rocker, facing the living room.

A column on each wall, with little cabinets below—glass doors now missing—marked the division between the dining room and the living room. Jim said his grandmother's long dining table stretched between those two columns, jutting into the living room. I remembered the oak table Dorothy Voelker had told me about, the one her daughter now had. I pictured it in the space and wondered how two caskets and mourners could squeeze into the living room, too.

But Jim remembered a sweet scent, one quite different from that of death. Grandma Pirkl had kitchen drawers and cupboards on the wall adjacent to the dining room. A swinging door once hung between the kitchen and dining room, and its top anchor remained visible on the jam. "Boy, I can still smell that door. That wood would hold that smell of that bakery. She'd have prune-and-apricot-filled poppy seed biscuits, some with dry cottage cheese and others with raisins and currants. Gees, that was good."

If Grandma Pirkl was baking at night, she did so by the glow of carbide gaslights. The lights were terrifically bright. But she had to be careful lest she'd blow up the place because the tank was buried next to the house and gas lines ran to each light.

The sink was still positioned so the user could gaze out the back window, just like when Grandma Pirkl watched Jim smack into Johnny's car. But Grandma's sink had no plumbing. Now, small cupboards atop the typical cupboards hide the pipes that were installed for the new sink.

In decades past, a sidewalk stretched toward the little barn that sheltered a buggy, as well as several horses; and later Johnny's car. But previous owners had torn down the barn 10 or 15 years earlier. In its place was a new garage.

When the Pirkls owned the place, there was an outhouse to the left of the walk. Behind the barn, next to the school, was a small fenced-in chicken coop, which housed just enough chickens to provide Grandpa and Grandma with eggs.

"Grandma grew moss roses thick along the sidewalk on the side, and they had a garden on both sides of the back sidewalk," Jim said. "They grew potatoes near the street and small veggies, popcorn, and sweet corn on the other side, so someone couldn't grab a radish or something as they walked past."

Jim recalled creating an ice rink on the lot to the north, across the road. "Us kids wanted a skating rink, so one winter we piled up snow in a circle and flooded it. In the spring, the ice all melted and somehow it flooded Grandpa's basement. That was the last skating rink we had there; he was a little perturbed about that deal."

Jim next explained that his grandparents had their bedroom on the first floor in the southeast corner of the house. A walk-in closet had doors from both the kitchen and the bedroom; space that is now filled by a bathroom. "Religious pictures hung over Grandpa and Grandma Pirkl's bed. They had little pinholes in the pictures. I don't know if bugs got in them or what. They had them at the farm and down at the townhouse, too; Christ, Joseph, and Mary. Ancient pictures; quite different."

There were two bedrooms upstairs. A roomy closet in the back corner was now a bathroom. The sturdy wood staircase is just as ever; perhaps Joseph Pirkl had crafted it. "If Grandpa built it, it was put together well," Jim said. "He didn't cut corners on anything."

After Grandma Pirkl died atop the steps leading to Dr. Joyce's dentist chair, the Pirkl home in Marshall was sold to Martha Langer, the woman who helped raise Cyril Langer, Johnny's best man; the same woman who helped Barbara Pirkl clean the clothes of Johnny and his bride after their accident.

The house would be remembered for being one of the last in the village to install indoor plumbing; and for a sad wake that followed, immediately, on the heels of a joyous wedding celebration.

A Hard Life

"Ed sat behind that wood box there, and he did drink."

"I always got in trouble with the guys."

During a chat at her home in Sun Prairie, Lila Labarro told how, as a high school freshman, she became the prom queen, dating the king, a junior, despite a teacher's objections, and how her marriage to Pete Labarro was short-lived because, "He went out a lot and met some other woman."

Lila's mother, Rose, was a sister of Josie Schuster, who married Johnny Pirkl's oldest brother, Ed. Lila, born in 1912—one of nine kids—recalled visiting the Ed Pirkl clan in Pine City. If Johnny and Hazel Pirkl had made it to Minnesota, they would have met with a situation less than idyllic for a honeymoon.

"Ed's family had a hard life," said Lila, who kept in close contact with her cousin Bernadine, Ed and Josie's daughter. The family called her Berdie.

"Ed always had a bottle in his hand," Lila said, matter-of-factly, while seated in her ranch home in Sun Prairie. "He was on the liquor. They did some dairy and some other farming but couldn't make a go of it. Ed sat behind that wood box there, and he did drink."

Lila was speaking from first-hand experience. "One year, Mom wanted to get out for the holidays. My brother Cy was manager at Oconomowoc

Canning in Stratford," she said of a town in north-central Wisconsin. "He was home for the holidays, so we drove back with him and used his car to go to Minnesota.

"We packed the trunk with canned corn and peas to give them something to eat," she said of her Pine City relatives. For mother and daughter, the trip was anything but a holiday. "It was so snowy, we didn't think we'd make it. We could barely get into Ed's driveway. We got there, and there wasn't a speck of fire heating the place. Josie went out with an ax to chop wood. Ed sat up all night."

Cy's car impressed his cousin Lawrence, youngest son of Ed and Josie Pirkl. "Lawrence wanted to take Cy's car to the tavern to show off all the gadgets. He begged. I wasn't sure Cy even had insurance on the car. I finally agreed but said I'd sit up waiting for him. He got home, and Josie was still out chopping wood.

"We slept with Josie. Mom said, 'I'll be so happy to go home. I don't think I'll ever want to go away again.'"

When Lila Labarro started painting a less-than-perfect picture of life in Pine City, I wanted to confirm the facts directly from Ed Pirkl's family. Lila and her cousin Bernadine wrote often and talked on the phone nearly every week. Occasionally, Bernadine would travel from Minnesota to visit Lila. I asked Lila to write or call me the next time Bernadine planned to visit, so I could plan a meeting.

The session never took place. I received word in March 1998 that Bernadine had died. She'd been living in St. Paul since retirement. Bernadine's memorial card stated she died March 9, which was a Monday. But Lila believed that date was incorrect.

"I talked to Bernadine about 10 p.m. Tuesday," she said of March 3. "I'd been asleep since 6 p.m. when she called. She said she needed heart surgery but was going to get a second opinion. I worried about her, so I called Friday and didn't get an answer. I called twice Saturday. I just never thought that woman had an ache or a pain; she was always happy. She probably went to church Friday morning. They found her in the bathroom, all red and blue. Her heart probably exploded. It says she died March 9, but I don't agree with that at all."

Lila knew it was a stretch to say Bernadine was always happy. You see, one thing in her life made her very unhappy, got her goat, and left her with heartache.

"She and Margaret didn't get along," Lila said of Bernadine and her older sister, Margaret Kluk. "She and her brother Lawrence were going to buy the family farm. But Lawrence was a terrible drinker. One night, he went out and never came home. He was killed in a car accident. Margaret was made administrator of the farm. Bernadine got real upset."

Bernadine and Lawrence had taken care of the farm, and Bernadine had put $12,000 into painting and fixing up the buildings. "After that," Lila said, "she never went out to Margaret's place."

This discussion of more family strife convinced me that I needed to talk with Margaret Kluk, the lone surviving child of Ed and Josie Pirkl. Lila told me Margaret, approaching her 80th birthday, was fighting cancer.

Margaret Kluk and her husband, Tony, lived in rural Brook Park, just a few miles northwest of Pine City. In March 1998, I wrote her a letter explaining why I'd be calling her.

"I am sorry to hear about the passing on of your sister Bernadine," I began. I explained that I was writing about Johnny and Hazel and wanted to include all relatives because family was so important to Johnny.

"And because Johnny and Hazel were on their way to see the Ed Pirkl family in Pine City when the accident happened, it's even more imperative to learn all I can about your family." I also added a primer regarding what I expected to be a delicate discussion: "From what I understand, it wasn't an easy life."

In our phone chat a couple of weeks later, we had talked only briefly about how her family came to settle in Pine City when Margaret opened up about her father's feelings. "My dad was not very happy up here because farming was so much different than it was when he was growing up, with it being colder and the growing season shorter. He liked southern Wisconsin farming much better. Of course, he had to break the land; there were just a few acres broken. He had to trim the trees to get it ready to plant, a lot of clearing to do."

Margaret recalled her father using sticks of dynamite to blow out stumps. "One time, he blasted a stump out by the woods, and a clump of dirt hit the roof of the house. He musta had a few too many sticks under that one. But he did get it all cleared off; there's just a little woods on it now. It was a lot of hard work.

"My mother didn't care to go back to Wisconsin. She liked it here. It made a little friction with he not caring for it here. But we had a nice place, a house and barn, a granary, and shop-shed."

She branched into other subjects before returning to the struggle of farm life. "It was hard, that's for sure. The Depression started on the farms in the late 1920s; that's when prices started going down. In the 1930s, Dad raised nice pigs. He had quite a few that he sold, and the price was so low he sold them to pay the taxes. He sold six or 10 and didn't get enough for them to pay the taxes because of the shipping costs. I remember he felt so bad about that and was so discouraged, which I can understand."

Later, Margaret willingly popped the cork on the subject of her father's drinking. "He overdid his alcohol," she said point blank. "I think it was depression. I think it was depression because he wasn't too happy here; the hard life, and I think he missed his family, too. They both were happy to go back to Wisconsin and visit their family," Margaret said of her parents.

By now, we were almost a half-hour into our discussion, and it had become apparent that getting the details to paint a true picture of life in Pine City would be much easier in person. Margaret broached the subject herself. "If you ever get up this way, I'd be happy to show you around," she said.

Some time passed before we arranged a meeting. I took an extra day off from work, and around 9 a.m. on a Tuesday in mid-November, I made the last turn onto a rural road—which soon changed from pavement to gravel—on my way to visit Margaret and Tony Kluk, who lived northwest of Pine City.

I stopped my pickup near the detached garage and climbed out, apprehensive of the farm dog's reaction. But surprisingly, the shaggy black and white canine wagged its tail and seemed to be friendly, even though it scampered away each time I attempted to pet it.

Tony Kluk greeted me at the door. The tall, strong-looking man invited me into the entryway, and it was immediately obvious that I was stepping back in time. A wood box, painted light green like the rest of the entryway, sat in the corner; a wine flask hung above it. Only later would the irony of that scene strike me, as I recalled how Lila Labarro described her Christmas visit to the Ed Pirkl farm.

I introduced myself, and Tony and Margaret invited me through the kitchen to sit at the dining room table, in a room adjacent to their living room. In the kitchen, a Round Oak wood-burning stove was radiating heat, the warm air filling the room. The white enamel and temperature dial on the oven door dated it newer than the old cast-iron models of Johnny Pirkl's day, but cracks divided two of the iron plates on its top, nonetheless. I could feel the slants in the floor as I walked. Still, pulling up a chair at the table, I felt at home in the comfortable surroundings, the furnishings in the dining and living rooms belying the home's age.

Ed Pirkl's only surviving child was about to tell me how the family came to settle in Pine City, while Ed's brothers and sisters remained in Dane County, Wisconsin.

I'd caught a hint of why Ed Pirkl came here when, months earlier, I'd visited Janice Weihert. Janice was part of the Johnson family and a neighbor of the Pirkls. She showed me a scrapbook that included obituaries of her grandparents, Vincent Johnson and the former Mary Hady. Janice's grandmother died at age 86 in 1939.

The list of survivors had bowled me over. Besides six daughters, two sons, 22 grandchildren, and eight great-grandchildren, Janice's grandmother was survived by a sister, Mrs. Joseph Pirkl of Marshall, and a brother, Michael Hady of Pine City. So the Johnsons and Pirkls were related, and Ed Pirkl had followed relatives to the Pine City region.

Lila Labarro thought Ed and Josie Pirkl might have first gone to the Dakotas to try farming before settling in Pine City. But Margaret Kluk said that was incorrect. "Grandma Pirkl's brother John Hady went to the Dakotas first, then came here to Pine City to be by his brothers, Mike and Tom," Margaret explained. "John was out on the prairie and said he wanted a place near trees and water. He got that."

John and his wife had three sons and three daughters. His youngest son, John, whom relatives called Pat, had an 89-year-old widow, Mildred, who was still living on the original Hady farmstead in Pine City.

Later, I climbed into Tony Kluk's white Olds Ciera SL. Tony was at the wheel, and Margaret sat in the back seat. I felt a bit uneasy with Tony driving. He was long past spry, and his laggardly reactions told me his driving days were nearly over. He seemingly took corners without braking, in countryside that was filled with swamps, creeks, and rivers.

We drove past the old John Hady place, a farmstead that didn't look as old as I expected. The farmhouse, certainly either refurbished or rebuilt from the original one, sat among a clutch of buildings at the end of a long driveway. It stood on a sort of plateau, somewhat hidden from the road by a lovely stand of mature hardwoods. Yes, Margaret was right. John Hady had found a place among the trees.

To the south, a bridge passed over Mission Creek, which trickled through a swampy area adjacent to the plateau. The Snake River, which couldn't be seen from the home, flowed behind the Hady place and intersected the neighboring property. The two waterways sandwiched the Hady homestead before they dumped into Pokegama Lake, just west of Pine City. Yes, John Hady got his water, too.

Margaret and Tony kept up a constant banter as Tony drove down gravel roads through farmland, swampland, and past woods before spilling onto Highway 11, approaching her home farm. The two kept pointing out places along the way.

"That farm's empty now," one would say.

"There's one that's still working," the other would reply.

"That house was built in 1994," one would say.

"That one went up last year," the other would add.

Indeed, it was a dog's lunch of properties: Abandoned barns and active farms, junky yards, and trailer homes interspersed with new homes—some sprawling, like former fields. It was just as Margaret had wistfully described on the phone: "Houses are going up all along that road. The farmers are almost all gone; very few farmers left around here. It seems like they don't want the small dairy farmers anymore, so you might as well get out of it, I guess.

"We remember the good old days when you knew all your neighbors. There's not so much neighboring going on anymore. People come and go; you get new neighbors all the time.

"In those days, they didn't farm so big like they do now. I don't know how that meat could be that healthful on big farms, with cows on top of manure piles. That's not the way God intended it. I don't know if this modern farming is going to be that good for us."

Tony pulled into the driveway of the former Ed Pirkl farm. A fine-looking two-story farmhouse stood to the left of a short driveway. On the right was a garage that appeared to have living quarters on the second floor. A couple of graceful, tall pines stood near the buildings. But branches of other trees hung naked on this dreary November day, ready for the wrath of another long, hard Minnesota winter, a season that—like an irritating relative—arrives too early and stays too long.

Margaret pointed to a pile of rubble through the trees and to the west of the garage. Those, she said, were the remains of her father's barn. Long gone were the corncrib and chicken house. The ravages of time also took the granary. It had stood close to Highway 11, to the right of the driveway. The highway once ran where the granary was later built. The road made an "S" pattern through her dad's farm. Ed Pirkl fought the government to get it straightened. The road crews did the job when she was three or four, but Margaret still remembered the project.

"I'd always come down to the cook's shed—she was cooking for the road crew—and she'd give me something to eat."

Tony added: "When you got a cookie or a piece of cake in those days, you'd appreciate it."

Margaret's father, with his Holsteins and workhorses, rode a train from Wisconsin to Pine City in late 1911, immediately after his wedding. A photo, likely snapped in 1912 or 1913, shows Ed, a stocky man of about five-foot-ten, standing by about ten Holsteins. His wide-brimmed hat is pulled down low on his face; a double-breasted coat covers his torso. Behind Ed and his herd stand a fine batch of buildings, a white, wood farmhouse, and red farm buildings with snappy white trim.

Her Grandpa Joseph Pirkl bought the farm from a fellow who had built up three farms in the area, Margaret explained. The house was new when Ed Pirkl arrived. A dozen or so Holsteins were kept on the farm in Pokegama Township, about 2½ or three miles west-northwest of Pine City. Along with the pigs and chickens, the Pirkls also raised geese.

Margaret's cousin Jim Benesch told me earlier how those geese were appreciated. "Uncle Eddie used to send a goose or two by railroad freight," Jim said. "Boy, Grandma made a good goose dinner."

Margaret recalled spending sunny summer days playing "house" in the chicken house with her siblings and helping her father pump the forge in his shed-shop. But all would not be rosy for long.

Margaret was born April 7, 1918; Anthony and Barbara came before her. Lawrence was born in 1920. Margaret still remembered the day of April 17, 1921: "My brother was a baby," she said of Lawrence. "Mom wanted to give him a bath and had a fire going. It was real windy. Dad had gone to town on horseback."

Similar to the way the Peck family home burned, ashes from the chimney ignited the wood shingles. "I was trying to help my mother," Margaret said. "Neighbors came over to help get stuff out of the house. She put Lawrence in the baby buggy and put us in the horse barn, and she made me watch him. Everyone was throwing things into the barn, on top of the buggy hood. I was worried they'd smother him. The next day, just the chimney was standing. They came and pushed it down because they worried it would fall and hurt somebody."

Rebuilding the farmhouse was no simple task because of the young family members. But Mike Hady and his family had gone to visit relatives in the Dakotas, so the Pirkls stayed at his place, a half mile down the road, until fall. "Then we lived in the granary for awhile," Margaret said. "It had been a house at one time, one room upstairs and one down. We got the house finished enough before it got cold so that we could move in the house and have a fire."

That wasn't the only fire that plagued the Ed and Josie Pirkl family. The couple's niece, Helen Josi, daughter of Leonard Springer and Martha Pirkl, recalled a blaze during one of the yearly "adventures" to visit the Pirkl family in Pine City.

"One time, for some reason, Dad and Ed were sleeping in the barn and it caught fire. I got so excited; I couldn't talk. All I could do was shake Grandma and point. They got out OK."

Fire wasn't the only struggle for Ed and Josie Pirkl. Margaret's father got pneumonia in the 1920s. "He almost died," Margaret recalled. "The doctors said he had a one-in-a-thousand chance of pulling through."

He did, but then it was Josie's turn. "My mother got sick in 1931. She was in the hospital three months with a bleeding ulcer. I stayed home from school one year to help her. I didn't start high school until the next year."

Her parents survived those ailments, and Margaret completed eighth grade at a country school, graduated from Pine City High School in 1936, and then she headed to the Twin Cities. She did housework for a while. Then she went to school for stenography and got a job in St. Paul with Montgomery Ward. Later, she joined Traveler's Insurance.

Like Ed Pirkl, Antoni Kluk and his Holsteins arrived in Pine County by train. Antoni and his wife emigrated from Poland and settled on the farm just up the road from where their son Tony now lived with his wife, Margaret. Only the barn still stood from the original Antoni Kluk farm. Tony was born in 1916 in Minneapolis. He farmed with his father until war broke out. In 1943, he was in the Army, manning artillery to defend the California coast. His view of potential enemy aircraft ranged ten miles.

But love was in the air, too. Tony Kluk's brother, Joe, worked for Ed Quiding, who'd married Margaret's sister Barbara. Joe introduced his brother Tony to Margaret Pirkl at a dance at the Crystal Palace in Pine City.

When Tony entered the service, it was supposed to be only for a year. But when the Japanese bombed Pearl Harbor, Tony was called to help secure the coast. "So most of our courtship was by mail," Margaret recalled.

Tony got home once or twice. Margaret went to California to visit him once. Not knowing if or when he might be shipped out, they decided to get married. She returned a second time, and on October 30, 1943, at St. Joseph in Berkeley, Tony Kluk wed Margaret Pirkl. Only Ed, one of Tony's three brothers, and Ed's girlfriend were there to witness the ceremony and support the newlyweds.

Tony and Margaret didn't wait long to start a family. Anthony was born in California the next August. "I got to see our baby before I left June 1," Tony said of the year 1945. "I was in Okinawa when they dropped the bomb on Japan. I was to be in the third wave invading Tokyo."

In 1946, Tony and Margaret bought their 120-acre farm. The house was only a 24-foot-by-24-foot structure. They later expanded it, adding on the back end, the front porch, and a second floor. In the next few years, using extra cash he got through armed services benefits, Tony built a chicken house, a granary to store feed and house livestock, a garage, and a barn. The barn was built in 1950, and the couple would be thankful for the metal roof that capped it.

Sitting in the driveway of the former Ed Pirkl homestead, Margaret pointed to a small stand of pines to the north, near the property line. Just beyond it stood her country grade school. Old-timers often boast of the miles they walked to school, but Margaret could get to her schoolhouse in short order. In fact, she could see it from her home.

But it's long gone. Like the original Pirkl farmhouse, fire destroyed the country school. The blaze hit the year Ed and Josie's youngest, Dorothy, graduated from eighth grade, around 1941.

The Pirkl farm buildings are gone, too, but several barn beams were salvaged and used to form an archway when the house was remodeled. John Mettling and his wife bought the house, garage, and the 48 acres on the south side of Highway 11. Kelly Osterdyke, who recently had been re-elected as zoning technician for Pine County, bought the 52-acre north half and built a home on it, Margaret explained. Neither worked the land; they left plowing, planting, and harvesting to farmers who rented the tillable acres.

Margaret expected that, someday, houses would be raised on the land her father once cleared with sweat and dynamite. And, she noted, Mettling and Osterdyke were classmates, friends and hunting buddies of Father David.

Margaret may have grown up under rough circumstances, but she and Tony raised a brood of well-adjusted children. "It was such a good place to raise kids," Margaret said of the farming community of Brook Park. "They learned responsibility; they had to work. You didn't have to worry about gangs and mischief; they were just too busy. Our kids all liked to study and got through on scholarships. All of our kids have done very well."

The war baby, Anthony, worked for the energy department in Maryland, inspecting nuclear plants for pollution and, if need be, shutting them down. The couple's six children were born in Minnesota, the last five at a former hospital in Rush City, about 11 miles due south of Pine City.

The couple was blessed with 19 grandchildren.

Margaret and Tony were duly proud of all their children, but perhaps they were most pleased with Father David. Born in 1956, he was ordained by Pope John Paul II in 1991. His parents displayed photos of his ordination day on their dining room wall. Additional snapshots from that memorable day in Rome fill an album. It was Father David, too, who built a little grotto for his parents on the south side of their white frame farmhouse.

Father David was with the Legionarios de Cristo in Mexico City, where he served as chaplain of a school. The children—all 2,000 of them—kept him busy.

Faith was important to Ed and Josie Pirkl, too. "My mother was very religious, and my dad was religious, too, but not as strong as she was," Margaret said. "My mother was a serious, studious person. Dad was kind of jolly, but sometimes he wasn't."

Ed and Josie attended Immaculate Conception Church in Pine City. The church spire pierces the sky a couple of blocks from the downtown area. Built in 1910, the red brick church is not unlike the architectural style of St. Mary's in Marshall. Those who objected to its demolition had recently thwarted a move to tear down the nearly 90-year-old church, Margaret said.

Like the surrounding countryside, Pine City was changing. A Wal-Mart was part of a shopping complex on the outskirts, and the usual collection of fast-food restaurants circled the city; the latest census indicated it was home to 2,613 residents.

Tony and Margaret Kluk celebrated their golden wedding anniversary in 1993. Even Lila Labarro attended the gathering, riding with her brother Jerome Blaska. "We stayed in a hotel nearby," Lila related. "Bernadine stayed with us in a big room. She got a cot to put in our room for ten dollars. She was scared of sleeping in the same room with Jerome. She had an earpiece to listen to the radio all night. It woke the others up.

"Bernadine led a very simple life. She had a one-room efficiency apartment but would never let me see it. We had to go elsewhere when I went to visit. She lived meagerly."

Animals no longer filled the buildings on Margaret and Tony Kluk's farm. Now, only the dog and two cats roamed the place. Tony and Margaret once milked up to 16 Holsteins. They used horses for many years to hold down costs, Margaret explained.

"We were quite frugal, like they say," Tony added.

Their farm had swamp and some woods, leaving only about 30 acres tillable. For 20 years, the couple rented another 120 acres, providing them with an additional 60 acres to till. They grew hay and oats, and they sold their extra alfalfa and straw.

Besides farming, Tony was a mail carrier, sometimes covering two routes. He milked cows until age 65. Then he raised beef cattle for a few years. He stopped delivering mail at age 70.

"We're retired now," Margaret said. "Just taking it one day at a time." In December, she noted, Tony would turn 82.

That's not too old to talk politics. What did he think of Minnesota's new governor—Jesse "The Body" Ventura—the former pro wrestler who'd body-slammed the national political scene by stunning well-known Republican and Democratic candidates in the gubernatorial race just two weeks earlier? Tony's reply was surprising. He'd voted for Ventura.

"I hate that old clique," he said of the politics-as-usual clutch at the Capitol. "Same old thing, year after year, and I thought a little change would do some good."

Tony and Margaret recalled another political discussion they'd had February 4, 1953. They were visiting her parents, celebrating her mother's 64th birthday, but her father was battling the flu.

"We were talking politics with my dad," Margaret reflected. "He was quite animated. He was lying down and visiting, but you could see he felt tired. But he didn't seem like he wanted us to leave. We stayed later than we'd expected to."

"He had been sick, but he didn't seem that bad that night," Tony said.

"But his heart was very bad," Margaret continued. "A neighbor came over the next day to tell us he'd passed away in his sleep. That was so hard to hear."

Josie Schuster Pirkl continued living on the farm until her death, at age 91, in 1980. She and her husband are buried in Birchwood Cemetery, Pine City.

Margaret's brother Lawrence was still living at the farmhouse, too. At one point, he milked up to 20 Holsteins before giving up farming and taking a job at a Purina feed store in Brook Park.

One April night in 1989, Lawrence was returning from Brook Park when he rounded a curve on Highway 11 and, less than a mile from home, collided with another vehicle and was killed. It was never clear which one crossed the centerline; perhaps both, Margaret said. A woman riding in the other car also was killed; her boyfriend suffered permanent back injuries.

"It was just one of those things," Margaret said. "Lawrence hadn't been feeling well. Maybe he had a slight heart attack. He had a couple of beers, but I don't think he was inebriated."

Lawrence was well-liked, and when Margaret and others started preparing food for the funeral, they were told to expect a big crowd, maybe 200 people. As it turned out, about 300 came to pay their last respects.

Later, with Lawrence gone, it was time to sell the old homestead, and Margaret confirmed the resulting clash with her sister Bernadine. "Berdie wanted to live in the old farmhouse," Margaret said. "But it needed lots of work."

Margaret recalled how, on a day years earlier, when Lawrence was at work, a teenage boy walked away from a nearby group home, entered the unlocked farmhouse and confronted Margaret's mother, demanding money. Josie Pirkl claimed she didn't have any. Finally, she gave him a dollar, telling him that's all she had. Fortunately, he accepted that and left. But the incident left Margaret and Tony fearful of Berdie's desire to live there.

"It was no place for an older woman living alone," Margaret said. "I wanted Berdie to take over administration of the property. She insisted that I do it, and then nothing I did was right. She was very unhappy with me."

Berdie sued the estate for $12,000, the amount she'd put into new siding on the house, Margaret explained. "I gave it to her instead of fighting it. Why give it to the lawyers?"

In a way, it seemed cold and callous to look a bit further into the death of Lawrence Pirkl. But most of this story is based on people's memories, some clouded through time, age, and circumstances. Here, however, was an incident in which police reports could offer factual information. How much alcohol had Lawrence consumed the night he died? Was his drinking coincidental to the accident, or did alcohol lead to his death, much like alcohol altered his father's life?

Chief Deputy Jerry Wedell answered my call to the Pine County Sheriff's Department. He didn't recall the accident at first, but after looking up the report, he realized that he had written it.

Wedell mailed me a copy of the report. A diagram shows that Lawrence Pirkl's vehicle wound up with its back passenger corner against the driver's side of a vehicle driven by 24-year-old Kelly Michael Potter of Grasston, Minnesota. Riding with Potter were Mary Alice Casper, 36, and Jack L. Gould, nine. Both vehicles wound up on the north edge of the highway. But some of the code numbers puzzled me, so I contacted Wedell by letter.

"Lawrence Pirkl and Mary Casper both died as the result of injuries sustained in this accident," he wrote back. "Lawrence's blood test showed a blood/alcohol level of .21. Legal intoxication, in Minnesota, is at the level of .10."

Wedell included a copy of information from the court administrator's office that included a case number of an apparent civil lawsuit, Kelly M. Potter vs. Margaret Kluk, administrator for the Lawrence R. Pirkl estate.

It was disappointing to learn that Lawrence tested as legally intoxicated because the accident killed two people. I opted to pursue the court records no further.

Bernadine's death nearly closed the book on the family name of Pirkl. Joseph and Barbara Pirkl of Marshall had raised a family of six children, so full of life, so full of promise. But it had dwindled and withered, much like the old way of farm life. Yes, many relatives survive. But their names are Benesch, Walker, Springer, Zimbric, Ramseier, along with a few others.

Johnny died without bearing children with the Pirkl name. Frank Pirkl and his wife, Helen, had two daughters, both of whom married into other family names.

Ed Pirkl and his wife, Josie, had three sons. Leslie Jerome was born blue in 1917 and died two weeks later. Lawrence never married. Only Anthony, born in 1913, had one son, Michael Pirkl, who lived in California, but his Aunt Margaret had no information on his whereabouts.

Margaret remembered another near tragedy; again, a fire, in 1976. This time, it nearly destroyed the farm where she and Tony raised their family. The blaze began west of their location under dry and windy conditions. Deer hunters may have triggered it. Firefighters dug a trench by the railroad tracks, but a wall of flames, 30 feet high, jumped the trench and raced across the parched land toward the Kluk farm buildings. The Kluks used both of their water pumps to spray down the buildings, the rooftops, and the grass.

"It was a frightful thing," Margaret said, recalling their horror.

"It's lucky we had a metal roof on the barn," Tony said.

Peat continued to burn a day later. With a 22-foot deep layer of peat below the railway, the tracks eventually sank. The next day, the smoldering fire ignited a dead pine tree behind the Kluk buildings, and firefighters had to return to save the place.

She was only nine at the time, but Margaret could reflect back on one other tragic day in her family. "We were all looking forward to seeing them," Margaret says of her Uncle Johnny and her new Aunt Hazel. "I remember it was such a gloomy day, dark, and rainy."

Winter seemed to be setting in especially early that fall; it had already snowed a bit. "But then we got this telegram that came to the depot. They delivered it right away, and it said they were both killed. It was a terrible shock. My dad, oh, he was so upset. He couldn't believe it. Dad went and got a train ticket and went down to the funeral. We were milking, so Mom had to stay. "It was so sad, to think their lives ended so suddenly."

Margaret had heard the story, passed on by relatives. "It was a terrible thing. You think of all the things you go through in life, and you never know."

Margaret reflected on her life, and she realized she missed out by not growing up closer to her Wisconsin relatives. "It was kind of lonely, in a way, without our grandparents around," she said. "We never got down to Wisconsin until we were older. We didn't get a chance to mingle with them."

She'd been to Wisconsin to visit when she was perhaps only three or four, but she recalled boarding the train in St. Paul and seeing a pool of water under the train. She was 18 or 19 at the time of her next visit by train. "We were farmers, you know. We didn't have a lot of time."

But Margaret remembered seeing Johnny's 1927 Chevy. "A couple of times, Grandpa drove that car up to visit us."

Margaret never expected to be the last survivor among her siblings. Anthony died in 1959. He was working on a tunnel project to divert water from the Feather River in the mountains in Nevada for use in California. He was preparing to leave work, making a final check. A locomotive was pushing carloads of dirt excavated from the project, and the engineer couldn't see Anthony walking on the tracks. Anthony, hard of hearing from years of construction work, never heard the train coming.

At the tender age of 19, Barbara married Ed Quiding, who was quite a bit older. She taught at a rural school for one year, had a daughter, Margo, and later returned to teaching. But Barbara had a liver problem, and that, coupled with too much medicine, apparently killed her in April 1965, as she was nearing the end of another school year.

Dorothy, a missionary nun out of an Irish order in Boston, was in Korea in the 1950s. Because she hadn't been there six months when her father died, she was not able to return for his funeral. Margaret remembered Dorothy's stories about how the missionaries were helping the Koreans. "People were so happy to see them. They'd come and bring their sick people, carrying them 20 miles on their backs. The Koreans were so poor . . ."

Dorothy died in 1982, just 29 months after her mother passed away. Besides Lawrence, Bernadine, and baby Leslie, Margaret had one other sibling who predeceased her: Frances Laura was born in 1919 and died a month later of pneumonia.

Margaret agreed that Bernadine's date of death on the memorial card was incorrect. A friend had stated that Berdie had attended Mass on Thursday and Friday. Berdie's groceries were put away, and she was fixing breakfast. "We figured it had to be Friday morning," Margaret said. "The coffee was on, an orange was on the table, the toast had been in. She started toward the bathroom. She fell as she came to the door. Her head was up against the tub, but she didn't hit the tub. She just collapsed like that. She was supposed to have triple-bypass surgery. She had an appointment that afternoon. She was so afraid of it, she was getting a second opinion. She never got there."

The fire burning in the Round Oak stove was to be the last one. Margaret and Tony planned to have new carpet installed in the entryway and kitchen the day after my visit. The installers would need to unhook the stovepipes and move the heavy old oven before laying the carpet. The stove, with one firewall cobbled together and its hot water well disintegrated, would remain outside. Margaret said she still occasionally used the oven, although she baked the cake and muffins she served to me in her Kenmore range. However, because Tony enjoyed splitting firewood, they'd probably install a newer wood-burner in place of the old wood stove. "Tony had congestive heart failure," Margaret had told me earlier. "He's kind of recovered. He can go out and chop up trees, which he likes to do. Our dog and two cats follow him wherever he goes."

Now the former dairyman, his farm wife, and their pets weren't wandering far from home. Margaret had not been able to attend the memorial service the previous fall that marked the 70th anniversary of the deaths of Johnny and Hazel. "I had to undergo chemotherapy every week," she said, and added that she had undergone colon surgery in April.

"I'm now off of it," she said of the treatment. "I guess I'm doing OK, but when you get to be this age, you tire out. I have to go back every three months to see the oncologist. They have to check you out. I have to do that for five years. I said, 'You think I'll live that long?' They said, 'Oh ya, you will. You've got good genes. I can tell by looking at you.'"

Margaret paused. "We never expected Berdie to pass away like that." More silence. "We'll take whatever comes."

I didn't ask if they planned to retire to a warmer climate. Sinking money into the place, installing new carpeting in the old kitchen, the answer seemed obvious. With three of their seven kids living around the nearby Twin Cities, this farm was home to Margaret and Tony Kluk.

The spat with Bernadine over money meant little, now that Berdie had died, leaving money to charities and some for Margaret and Tony. Maybe the argument, I reckoned, was really about the loss of heritage, the selling of the old homestead. Maybe it was Berdie's desperate attempt to cling to the past, to preserve the way of life she was born into, to gather a few rocks for a flower garden, so to speak. I could appreciate and relate to those feelings.

Before leaving, I asked Margaret and Tony to step outside so I could snap a picture of them. They slipped on jackets and did so. "Now pretend like you know each other," I teased. They chuckled and responded that they "guessed they did." They put their arms around each other, smiled, and I clicked. In turn, they took my picture.

They asked when my research would be complete. My reply troubled even me. I explained that I was one year into a five-year plan. Disappointedly, they expressed doubt that they would be around to read the story. As I started down the dusty gravel road, I hoped they were mistaken.

Johnny Drives Away Proud and Tall

"The most beautiful Chevy ever built"

The automobile revolutionized life in America, and Johnny Pirkl was the first in his family to realize its value. By 1920, more than eight million cars were traveling a patchy network of roads that did not meet the needs of drivers. Automobiles opened the door to new kinds of recreation, distant vacations, and better job opportunities. Autos helped erase the isolation of farm life, narrowing the gap between rural and urban lifestyles.

Autos also changed the shape of courtship. If Johnny had a car, he could take his bride-to-be to a distant community to "kick up their heels" to a dance band, and, if they so chose, they could stop afterward at a secluded place and enjoy moments of passion in the back seat.

In the last half of the decade, Henry Ford's Model T was losing its grip on the low-priced car market. People were not content to drive slow-moving Fords—in designs and colors that some people considered ugly—while the more-colorful Chevrolets sped past. Ford didn't unveil its Model A until December 2, 1927. It's not surprising that Johnny Pirkl turned his attention to the Chevrolet dealer in Marshall.

Ed Strasburg and Julius Packel opened an automobile dealership on Marshall's Main Street in 1915. This information was compiled for the

Marshall Historical Society by the late Postmaster Stan Trachte. When Frank J. Lazers returned from a three-month World War I stint in the Army, he bought the Marshall Motor Company from Strasburg and Packel. Lazers sold Johnny Pirkl what likely was the family's first car; a dark gray 1927 Chevrolet Capitol Series AA coach.

Catherine Lazers Bauer was the only child of Frank and Annie Lazers and wrote a fictional news story about Bridal Pond. In her 1999 book, *One Day On Earth, a Third Eye View*, she describes her roly-poly father as a happy and optimistic Bohemian. He loved pulling pranks on Halloween trick-or-treaters and whistling at pretty girls. His daughter was his frequent companion at the circus, Chicago Cubs games, on fishing trips, and while shooting clay pigeons with a .410 gauge shotgun. Frank bought his daughter a tiny Austin automobile when she turned 10. That's right—10. His wife was horrified.

Frank Lazers "chose to overlook 'minor flaws' and celebrate the positive, whether in buildings, in people, or in the affairs of everyday life," his daughter wrote. This upbeat outlook was in spite of severe burns, which he had sustained in a gasoline explosion in 1951. The accident left him with no lines on his face and with skin as pink and smooth as an infant's. " 'Life is what you make it,' he used to say, and he practiced what he preached by making his own life merry."

It struck me that people described Johnny Pirkl in much the same way.

The Lazers family lived in the small gray bungalow Frank built across the alley, behind his Chevy dealership. Unless he went on vacation, Frank never locked the doors of their home—a house that had many imperfections. The kitchen floor slanted, and Bauer wrote that an upstairs hallway wall had ripples and swells resembling a fun-house mirror. The dirt-cheap kitchen cupboards had shelves covered with varnished plywood doors with small holes cut out where door pulls should have been. The jerrybuilt house was not unlike the dealership, which was also pieced together like a patchwork quilt, as Frank could afford to make improvements.

Lazers' dealership consisted of two buildings that were attached to each other. Originally the office was close to the street and adjacent to two gasoline pumps—one taller than the other. Later, Lazers built a canopy over the area. In 1928, he put an addition on the west side to house an office and two bays where the mechanical work was done.

It was this latter arrangement that I recall from my boyhood trips to visit my Grandpa and Grandma Klecker on Pardee Street. While standing in Grandma's raspberry patch, I could almost look through the drive-in repair shop. I would often cut across the oily gravel alley and stroll past mechanics to the front office where I'd find my grandfather sitting with his cronies. On warm, sunny days, they would move outside to a shaded bench. I could often talk Grandpa into buying me an Orange Crush or a Grape Nehi, and I'd pull the seven-ounce bottles from a well of cold water inside the Coca-Cola pop machine. I don't recall ever seeing another soda machine quite like it.

For 13 years, Frank Lazers proudly served as village president, and he conducted much of the village's business from his garage office. He was supportive of sports programs, and, for years, he sponsored the Marshall Lazers Motors baseball and basketball teams. He commanded the American Legion for 12 years, " . . . so loyal you'd think he'd won World War I all by himself," his daughter wrote. He served as pallbearer for many funerals, she noted, and always furnished a car for the mourners. His Chevy dealership was, for many years, one of the largest in the state. His final years brought heart trouble, diabetes, and hardening of the arteries, leaving him in foggy senility. Yet he didn't retire until 1972, only one year before he died at age 81.

In 1926 or 1927, Johnny Pirkl arrived at Lazers Motors, likely by horse and buggy. When he left, he was driving a shiny new car. Johnny's relatives have no information on the date of the transaction or on the price he paid for the vehicle. The answers perhaps lay among the thousands of receipts and records, musty and crumbling like leaves that, for decades, sat stuffed in dusty banana boxes; stored where mice scurried above the more recent businesses housed in the former Lazers Motors building. Perhaps record of the sale was pitched out years later with boxes left soggy by a leaky roof.

History shows that Chevrolet manufactured nearly 240,000 of the two-door coupes that year and priced them at $695. Engineers from Chevrolet and Fisher Body teamed up to boost sales by creating fresh styling on the Capitol Series AA cars, billed as "The most beautiful Chevy ever." Beneath the quality trimmings sat the same mechanical package as Chevrolet used for its K and V series cars. The car weighed 2,190 pounds and was a pinch longer than 148 inches. Underneath the metal body panels was a frame built with wood parts, just like the other Fisher bodies manufactured by the Detroit corporation between 1926 and 1934. The frame measured a tad wider than 44 inches in back.

Under metal covers that opened on each side of the automobile lay a four-stroke engine that produced a maximum 26¾ horsepower. The car had 29-inch balloon tires and rear drum brakes. It came equipped with a ten-gallon gas tank that was mounted next to the spare tire on the back.

The interior was advertised as having room for five passengers, although fitting three in back would be a "squeeze," especially by today's standards.

Johnny drove away proud and tall. He made sure several photographs had been taken of his new car before the day he drove away from St. Mary's Church, his new bride at his side.

I could see the irony in this. I was in search of a 1927 Chevy Capitol Series AA—to analyze, to sit in, and to listen to the sound of its engine. Yet I used the Internet for my search. In March 1998, I hit a bull's-eye on the World Wide Web: A classified advertisement on the "Classic Car Source" sought a buyer for a 1927 Chevy. I determined from the area code that the seller lived in northern Minnesota; not a location just around the corner, but, at least, in the Midwest.

I called the owner, Josh Dahl, of Bagley, Minnesota; a town about 250 miles north of Minneapolis. I told him I wasn't interested in buying the car but rather in examining it. He mentioned that his daughter lived in Rockford, Illinois, and Interstate 90 took him past Janesville on his trips to visit her. But, of course, he didn't drive the vintage car on those trips. I indicated that I would attempt to locate a similar car in the Janesville vicinity, and that I'd check back with him in a few months in the hope that someone closer to Janesville had perhaps bought his car.

Meanwhile, I contacted two Midwest auto museums as well as the sponsors of an annual antique auto rally. I talked to people in the antique-auto hobby. I scanned publications dealing with old cars, and I called an editor. There were no leads on any other 1927 Chevy.

I contacted Josh Dahl again. He still had the car. I explained that, before driving that distance to see it, I wanted to confirm that it was the model I was in search of. General Motors made several models in 1927. Among these were the 1927 Chevrolet Capitol Series AA coupe and coach. I was convinced, judging from photographs, that Johnny had owned the coach—the one with the rear seat and squared-off back end. Josh said that my description matched that of his car. At my request, he agreed to send me a few photos. Weeks passed, and I did not hear from him.

I called again. Josh explained that he had been busy. He also said he'd had the car tuned up and intended to store it for the winter. I decided to take action. I mailed him photocopies of my two pictures of Johnny's car. I called him in early November, and he indicated that his car was the "match" I was looking for.

I figured I would make a triangular trip. I could visit my brother Ed in Minneapolis and use his place as headquarters for a Sunday-Tuesday excursion to see Margaret Kluk in Brook Park and Josh Dahl in Bagley.

I hoped the weather would cooperate. A major storm blew through the Midwest on November 10, bringing back memories of the November gale that sank the Edmund Fitzgerald on Lake Superior a couple of decades earlier, inspiring Gordon Lightfoot's haunting ballad about the freighter. The current storm had knocked out power, downed trees, blew roofs off buildings, and dumped snow in northern regions. If the weather became too inclement, I'd have to postpone the trip until spring. This was the time of year when the weather generally worsened; and, in Minnesota, winter seemed to last forever.

On Sunday, November 15, I headed for Minneapolis. The roads became slick as I approached the city, so I kicked my Ford Ranger into four-wheel drive and made it to Ed's home, safe and sound. Next stop, Bagley, Minnesota.

Sunday night's weather reports for northern Minnesota were less than ideal. Overnight snow was forecast for the Bagley area. It didn't sound bad enough to keep me off the roads, but it might slow me down. The bigger question: Would Josh want to take his antique auto out on sloppy roads? I was apprehensive about that, and I also wanted to double-check all plans before driving the many miles. It was my intention to be on the road by 7 a.m. in order to beat the Twin Cities' rush-hour traffic and arrive in time to see the car, get my questions answered, and return to Minneapolis by suppertime.

On Monday, I called Josh on a cell phone at about 8:30 a.m. As I dialed his number, the irony struck me again—modern-day technology was serving as my link to a 1927 automobile.

Josh confirmed the snowy situation, but he assured me that he'd be waiting for me. "Take your time," he said. "I'll be here all afternoon."

I made good time until I got to Wadena, more than an hour south of Bagley, where the roads became hazardous. By the time I turned onto Highway 200, I thanked God for four-wheel drive. Several inches of snow still blanketed the highway. Plows were nowhere in sight, and every vehicle coming toward me seemed to be a logging truck bearing a heavy load. Had I been traveling in a two-wheel pickup, I'd probably have wound up splattered to the bumper of an 18-wheeler like a summertime mosquito.

I felt like I was in Canada as I neared Bagley. In reality, I was hours south of the border. Josh gave me simple directions to his place, and, before noon, I was pulling up his hilly driveway.

Josh was coming down the drive in another vehicle. He waved, and we stopped near his garage and greeted each other. I immediately liked this personable fellow.

A minute or two later, he hopped in my truck and we were off to Roger Ranisate's place, where, at the end of a row of vehicles, under a blue tarp—with a half-foot of snow atop it—I spotted a sharp, medium green 1927 Chevy Capitol Series AA coach. I was excited to see it. I wanted to take this relic home and shelter it in my garage against winter.

Josh brushed the snow off the car, and Roger came out of the house as Josh and I were peeling back the tarp. It was frozen to the leather-like roof material. I seemed more concerned than Josh about damaging the top as we removed the tarp.

I snapped a few pictures. The exterior was in decent shape with only a few spots of rust. Josh guessed that the paint was original. It seemed to me it had to be either black or gray. I noticed the Chevrolet nameplate—the same two-winged logo that still adorns Chevys.

Roger jumped in and fired it up. Amazingly, it came to life in just a second or two. He obviously knew his stuff.

"Hop in and take it for a drive," Josh suggested. The offer floored me and made me anxious. I did not expect to drive the car. Riding along with Josh would be satisfying enough. I wasn't sure I knew enough about the unfamiliar controls to take it for a spin.

"How about if I ride along while you drive it, and I'll take the wheel on the way back?" I replied. Josh agreed. We stepped onto the running boards, climbed in, and closed the doors, which seemed to work somewhat awkwardly. Josh gripped the smooth metal ball atop the stick shift on the floor, pulled it into first gear, and eased out the clutch. The car lurched forward. We headed down the snow-covered back road, Josh positioning the skinny six-inch tires in the tracks left by a previous vehicle.

Ruuuu-gaaahhhhh! Josh had hit the horn, and the resulting sound jogged memories of summertime parades. We chuckled.

In third gear, the car started to chug, so Josh downshifted to second. Gas fumes enveloped us, and I thought they'd be enough to make one ill on a long trip, say, from Marshall to Portage. But perhaps the fume problem was due to the busted out back window, the shards of glass still covering part of the hole. Apparently Josh's grandson had recently broken the window when he rolled it down. Josh hadn't had time to order a new pane.

Soon we came to a "T" in the road, and Josh turned around. We exchanged seats and started back down the road. Unfortunately, there were no tracks to follow on this side, and I felt the car sliding toward the shallow ditch. I edged the car over into the existing path.

"I think I'll keep it over here," I said. I was driving on the wrong side of the road, which, on this day, was not a problem because the 1927 Chevy was the only car on the road.

As I drove, my mind turned to the accident that had ended the lives of Johnny and Hazel. Driving a car identical to Johnny's provided a clear picture of what must have happened.

The car had no seat belts. My knees were riding high, my butt low. If the car hit something, heads would strike the windshield or the roof. A lone, narrow wiper blade reached down from its mount atop the windshield to clean only a small area of glass on the driver's side. The car had no defroster. I realized that, as darkness fell on that fog-shrouded evening in 1927, the new Mrs. Pirkl probably never saw what was coming.

I shifted into third gear. Something was amiss. Either that or it would have taken a lifetime to get from Marshall to Pine City.

We were back, and as I slowed to turn in, I realized the brakes were designed for slow, easy stops. Johnny Pirkl never had a chance.

I backed the car into the spot, and we laughed at how the key seemed to pop out of the ignition, like a jumping bean, when the engine was turned off.

We got out, and Josh unhooked the two latches on the driver's side of the engine cover, grasped the little handle, and lifted the hood. The engine block was more rusty than the exterior, but it was not in bad shape for its age. A plate on the cab wall read, in part: Fisher Body Corp., Detroit, Mich.

A mechanic, I'm not, so I snapped a photo as Josh named and explained each part: The gas manifold, vacuum line, fuel pump, fuel line and filter, generator, breather cap—with little holes for the pipe leading to the oil pan—and a spot for adding grease, or "hard oil" as they used to call it, for the water pump.

We repeated the exercise on the other side: Horn, exhaust pipe, distributor with wires for the four spark plugs, and starter with a soup-can sized coil for voltage.

The spare tire was centered between the bumper and the window, the Minnesota license plate in the middle of it. I remembered that those who discovered Johnny and Hazel saw only the spare and the sign indicating Lazers Garage. Left of the spare was the cap for the ten-gallon gas tank, and to the right of the spare was the gas gauge. I chuckled at the spelling "EMTY."

I snapped several photos of the dash and the foot pedals. I thought it funny how small the clutch and brake pedals were—identical horizontal ovals with small nubs to keep one's foot from slipping. The round, small gas pedal, not much bigger than a silver dollar, was to the right.

Josh explained the gauges, buttons, and gadgets. The round odometer showed a top speed of 75 mph, but he figured the upper limit would be closer to 60 mph. The mileage stood at 81179; we couldn't tell if that meant 81,179 or 8,117.9 miles.

Josh was a bit puzzled when I asked about the two metal levers in the middle of the steering wheel; one read "closed" and the other "advance." He set off to ask Roger, and I continued to explore the car's interior. Light green fabric, which seemed to be original, covered the seats and the doors.

The front seats flipped forward in two steps—first the back tipped, then the bottom flipped, allowing passengers access to the back seat.

A black shade rolled down to cover the back window, if need be. I wondered if Johnny and Hazel ever "parked," and rolled down such a shade.

I joined Josh and Roger in the shop, where Roger explained that the "advance" lever provided spark to smooth out the ride in third gear, and the "close" lever was for throttling down again. This explained why the Chevy ran so rough when we shifted into third.

Besides flushing out the engine, Roger had rebuilt the starter and installed a new battery and positive ground cables. Roger was an experienced mechanic. He had spent 25 years working outside Boston. Later he worked on big trucks and cars at a Chevy dealership in Bemidji, about 25 miles from Bagley.

"I got too old and too tired to work on those big, old trucks," he said in his high-pitched voice. "That's why I put in an eight-foot door here."

Roger said he had driven a few old cars, a Model A and a Model T among them. "This is probably the oldest car I've ever worked on."

Josh said a 1931 Chevy was his first car, adding that the '27 Chevy is "a year older than I am."

The two trim old-timers got a bang out of talking about the hand crank in front of the '27 Chevy, the one you stuck in a slot below the radiator and turned when the starter was stubborn. You cranked by pulling up, so that if it backfired, and the crank pitched backward, it slipped off your fingers instead of breaking your wrist or your thumb. Many young fellows broke bones while hand-cranking old tractors. "If you have one guy on the crank and one on the starter inside," Roger added, "it won't backfire."

Before we left, I snapped a picture of Josh in the car. He suggested that he take my picture, so we traded places. My grin, as captured by the camera, revealed my sense of satisfaction with my trip to northern Minnesota.

Josh and I stopped for lunch in town and headed back to his place. I sat at a snack counter in his kitchen, while he looked for the paperwork on the car. As I perused my notes, I admired his comfortable, airy home with the cathedral ceiling, generous amounts of exposed wood, and lots of windows to the world.

Josh returned with the title, and I jotted down the details while he brewed a pot of coffee. The last owner was Oliver Solt of Solway, a hamlet on Highway 2 between Bagley and Bemidji. Oliver's son Jack owned the car, Josh explained. Jack had worked as a dragline operator, but, one spring, his boom touched overhead power lines, and the resulting jolt killed him.

Josh had owned the car 14 years, acquiring it in a series of business deals. The Chevy sat for years in an old shed on his property. Josh said he had never put the car in parades. "My wife likes it when we drive it around," he said.

His grandchildren weren't so interested in the General Motors relic. "The grandkids like four-wheelers and snowmobiles."

When Josh tore down the collapsing sheds, he lost storage space for the car. He planned to drive it home later that day and rig up some sort of shelter for it.

"A collector of Chevys said he thought it was worth $10,000," Josh said. "A year ago, he'd have bought it from me. But now, he sold all his Chevys and collects John Deere tractors."

If I had an interest in buying the car, Josh offered to deliver it to me for $7,000 at Thanksgiving when he would be driving to Rockford. I wished I had that much to spare.

The Story of "Kay"

"When we heard about the accident, we were stunned."

The dust of bachelorhood covered the dark cherry wood on the Poole piano. The piano, built in Boston, sat in the corner of the living room farthest from the front door. The display of photos on the piano told the story of a family.

So did Lawrence Conrad, who sat in a rocking chair. He often folded his weatherworn hands; other times, they stroked his stubble-filled chin. He spoke with an impediment; perhaps that was the reason, I thought, he never married. He was a congenial gentleman. I had to listen carefully to hear his story of "Kay."

"Kay." That's what he called his oldest sister, Catherine, the maid of honor at Johnny and Hazel's wedding. Catherine had lived in this house in Sun Prairie. Lawrence was about 15 when Hazel was stopping to visit Catherine to plan the wedding.

I asked Lawrence how his sister happened to know Hazel, thinking, maybe, they had both attended Sun Prairie schools. They weren't school-mates, he told me. Johnny actually knew Catherine first. Perhaps they had met at a street dance, where cornmeal was spread to make the dance area slippery; or maybe at the pavilion at Angell Park; or in the dance hall above Conrad's Restaurant on Main Street, where Romp's Korner Inn was now located. Catherine got to know Hazel when the couple started to date, Lawrence stated.

The Conrad home at 122 Vine Street had a small front porch with pillars and spindles on the railing; shorter, decorative spindles wrapped around the roof line of the house. Otherwise, it resembled the typical farmhouse from a century or more ago. Now, it looked out of place, sitting behind the grand, new Sun Prairie Municipal Building, which spread across the 300 block of Main Street. Police squad cars sat in the parking lot next to the Conrad property line.

The burgeoning city grew up around the two-story wood-frame house, pushing it aside. Decades ago, the house sat about a block to the west. It was moved to make way for a new post office, a facility that, in turn, made way for an even newer post office. But the Conrad house remained, even though the city tried to buy the property, raze the house, and expand the municipal lot, as Lawrence explained.

But he had no intention of selling. He couldn't sell it; not the home he'd grown up in; a house that held so many memories. He reckoned the city would get it soon enough, when he was gone. For now, he was content to sit in the hand-carved wooden rocker, recapping a colorful life and the story of Kay.

Catherine Alice Conrad was born January 13, 1905. She was the oldest of six children born to Henry Conrad of Sun Prairie and piano teacher Dora Luegers. Dora hailed from the town of Columbus, 12 miles northeast of Sun Prairie.

Al was born in 1909, Lawrence in 1912, and Eugene in 1914. Another girl, Mary, was born in 1916, and Dorothy came in 1919.

Henry Conrad was a studio photographer. His business was on Main Street, just a few steps from their home. The municipal building stands there today. Henry had to do more than shoot photos to keep eight bellies full. He also sold musical instruments.

"Things were tough back in the Depression," Lawrence remembered. "You'd make 22 cents an hour—if you could get a job—and you held onto every damn cent you had. My dad was selling pianos and Victrola phonographs. Then, radio came along, and—overnight—no more piano sales.

We figured if we put in a grocery store, at least we'd get groceries wholesale."

A couple of years before the Great Depression, Conrad's Grocery was squeezed into the building that housed the photo studio. It's not to be confused with the other Conrad grocery, owned by Joe and Carl Conrad, cousins of Lawrence and his siblings. Joe and Carl later opened a Sentry grocery.

Ironically, the outbreak of World War II was a blessing to Henry Conrad's family. "Nobody had any money," Lawrence reflected. "We didn't know what the hell to do. Along comes the war, and every young fella had to have his picture taken, and Dad was taking pictures day and night. That's the only thing that made us survive."

The Conrads were educated at nearby Sacred Hearts Catholic School. Catherine finished the eighth grade. Then she learned shorthand, typing, and banking in a two-year commercial course. She could have gone into banking, but instead she took a job with the local water and light commission. That's why three similar ornate metal light fixtures still hung from the ceilings in the Conrad home. Catherine bought the fixtures—each with a trio of dangling bulbs—at half price. One fixture hung in the kitchen. Another was suspended from the ceiling in what was now Lawrence's bedroom. The third formed one point of a triangle with Lawrence's rocker and the old piano.

Photos were lined up on the piano. One showed an attractive young woman, Catherine, in her late 20s. Lips with off-red lipstick framed her pretty smile, which created a slight dimple. Her spiral-like earrings resembled seashells. Short, wavy brown hair was parted on the right, and her bangs were swept up.

Catherine would have been a "fine catch" for any young suitor. But many who tried to get to know her were destined to fail. Maybe it was the memory of Johnny and Hazel that made her reluctant; or possibly it was her strict Catholic upbringing. She had dated Cyril Langer, who stood up opposite her at Johnny and Hazel's wedding. But the relationship never went anywhere.

"She was a tough one. She always had boyfriends. She'd meet up with all these fellas working on the highways. She was a funny girl. She had boyfriends, but they were just friends. There was no sexual thing,"

Lawrence said matter-of-factly. "No romantic stuff. They'd just go out in the boat and sing."

All the Conrads sang. They'd sit on the screened side porch—now a dilapidated structure that faced the municipal building—and they would sing while swaying in the double-seat swing. Catherine had a ukulele with 12 strings. It was called a Tippell. "A helluva nice instrument."

Music was important in the Conrad family. Despite his mother's tutoring, Lawrence was not adept at the keyboard, but the snare drum was another story. By the time he turned 18, he played in the Marshall and Sun Prairie bands with his trumpet-playing father.

Catherine played the violin, but not in local bands. On weekends, she was too busy tending the grocery store, checking out customers, and restocking shelves.

When she wasn't sitting on the side porch, or minding the store, she was out with a handful of lady friends such as Antoinette Klein and Lila Labarro. "They'd go on picnics and play beautiful music," said Lawrence. He searched his memory for the names of songs: "Whispering Hope," "My Old Kentucky Home," "My Wild Irish Rose," "With Someone Like You," "It's a Long, Long Way to Tiparari," and "Drifting and Dreaming." They were beautiful songs, ones with melodies and meanings, unlike the rock music of today, he said, with a tinge of disgust.

Years later, Catherine would return to Sacred Hearts to fill the church with memorable string melodies during midnight Mass on Christmas Eve. "They'd have a violin duet," Lawrence recalled with a distant look that made me believe he could still hear the music. "It was beautiful."

Lila Labarro recalled her old friend, Catherine, as just that—an old friend. "She didn't get out and go with any people of her own age at all," Lila remembered. "I would just call her an old maid at that time. When I was in high school, I picked her up to do things, go to church meetings, and things like that. She didn't go to many dances."

Eventually, Catherine moved to Milwaukee, where she bought a house and worked as a secretary for the Federal Housing Administration. At age 38, she met Thomas Willmes, a man Lawrence recalled as being about six years younger than she was.

Catherine Conrad, above, was Hazel Ferguson's maid of honor. Right, Her younger brother, Lawrence Conrad, in 1998. Below: Lawrence Conrad's home in downtown Sun Prairie.

Thoughts turned to love. But her Catholic upbringing, which forever kept sex a secret, had Catherine perplexed, as Lawrence explained it. He said she went to Sister Charissima—principal at Sacred Hearts and, ironically, the aunt of Thomas Willmes—to ask a startling question: "If I hold a boy's hand, does that mean I'm gonna have a baby?"

Catherine and Tom wed but never had children. Tom, a distributor for Canada Dry, was a soldier in World War II. He had fought in France and was wounded in the Battle of the Bulge. Apparently his injury prevented the couple from having children.

Catherine and Tom sold Catherine's house in Milwaukee to buy a restaurant in downtown Racine. "That's when everything went to hell," Lawrence recalled. "Tom was happy-go-lucky. He liked to 'tip a few,' play pool, mix in with the boys." A slim, handsome fellow with reddish hair, "He liked to show off if he had a little money." The fact that he was younger than Catherine, "That's where the trouble came in," Lawrence said.

The restaurant had no parking, making business a tough go. The restaurant was a joint venture with Tom's brother and his wife, who later talked Tom and Catherine into buying them out. Catherine and Tom asked Lawrence and his brother Al for a $3,000 loan.

Lawrence worked at Sun Prairie's Wisconsin Porcelain—the company where my friend Mike Taylor worked in his younger days and whose owner once owned the Ferguson farm. A tiff with his supervisor sent Lawrence back to the grocery, which he ran from 1949 to 1960.

"There were about six grocers trying to make it on Main Street at the time. I worked 8 a.m. to 11 p.m., 365 days a year. The priest didn't like it that I stayed open on Sundays and holidays. But we'd get fresh bread from Gardner's and pack the store on weekends." The Sunday crowds shopping at the lone open store kept the cash register ringing.

Al, meanwhile, was a surveyor for Dane County. He eventually talked Lawrence into closing the grocery and going into surveying, which they made into a successful business.

Al and Lawrence gave Catherine and Tom the money they needed, but it didn't help. The restaurant in downtown Racine eventually closed.

However, Catherine and Tom didn't give up on the idea of food service. They bought two or three acres on the outskirts of Racine and built a nightclub.

"Tom, he was in with the boys, having drinks, playing pool, going bowling," Lawrence repeated. "Kay and Tom were never meant for each other. He was a city boy. They ran this place, but it never paid off."

When Tom and Catherine needed more money to keep the place running, Al and Lawrence sent it. "They'd come and visit, buy a crate of eggs, and use the trip as a tax write-off."

Lawrence and Al were given shares in the nightclub. Later, the interest payments on the loans stopped coming. "I told Tom we needed the interest payments. He said, 'If we've got to start paying interest, we'll have to shut down.' We wrote it off. We never said anything more about it.

"They'd get a polka band in from Racine, and people'd come in and listen but not spend much. And the band didn't get paid much but got all the free brandy they wanted. They were always spending more than they had," Lawrence said of Tom and Catherine. "You'd think, running a business with no children, they'd make money. But damn it, they couldn't make it.

"Kay always had highfalutin ideas, always bigger than reality. That's why they never made it. And she was tougher than hell. Al and I always said we'd feel sorry for whomever she'd marry because she'd be the boss. It was rough on Tom. She was dominant. She took over. She decided where they were gonna live. But she was real good-hearted, to a fault."

By the early 1970s, Catherine decided to retire in northern Wisconsin. They began looking for a spot. Finally, in 1972, they bought 120 acres in the Washburn County town of Brooklyn and had a wood-frame prefabricated Wick home built. They sold the nightclub for $75,000, as Lawrence remembered. "She had a dream world idea," Lawrence recalled. "She thought Al and I could sell out and move up there, and Al could go hunting."

Catherine and Tom lived in rural tranquility, but Tom was out of his element in the north, Lawrence said. "She liked trees, and they had a meadow near the home where they could watch deer. She was the boss. He was never meant for that type of life, being from Milwaukee. He let her know, toward the end. He wasn't drawing Social Security yet. That kind of life wasn't for him. They got along all right, but it wasn't too peaceful."

Tom died in early 1981.

Catherine's sister Mary paid her a visit in May 1984. As Mary and her husband prepared for their trip home, Catherine asked them to fill the gas tank on her Ford Grenada and to park the car in her basement garage. They carried out her wishes. Soon after, an electrical short started a fire.

Catherine hustled to the phone and called the fire department. Smoke detectors blared as she hurried out the door, grabbing her chest and mumbling something about her heart. She fell. Firefighters were ten minutes from the scene.

"The fire happened on Memorial Day," Lawrence recalled. "The fire department had a new truck and an old truck. The new one was in a parade in Minong, so they sent the old one. It ran out of water, of course.

"Al and I got a call from Mary," Lawrence remembered, vividly. "She said, 'Catherine's gone, the house is gone, and we want you up here right now.'"

Catherine Conrad Willmes died tragically, like her friends Johnny and Hazel, on May 30, 1984. She was 79.

Lawrence sat in the dark wooden rocker that was his brother's favorite. He used to sit in the old cushion chair next to the piano, and Al sat in the 100-year-old rocker with the ornate wood trim and handle to tilt it back. Lawrence never understood why Al liked the chair so much until his brother died in 1995, only three years after they gave up their surveying business. The chair became Lawrence's favorite.

The home looked much like it did decades earlier—as Catherine would have remembered it: An older model television sat in the living room, where a wooden picture rail ran around the walls, several inches below the ceiling. In the kitchen, vinyl runners, with worn or broken-off edges, covered the hardwood floor, and Al's fishing reels leaned against a doorframe—giving the impression that the brothers were contemplating going out "to drown some worms." The roots of a mature maple tree had buckled the concrete slabs of the driveway.

The short tour was completed, and Lawrence returned to his spot in "Al's" chair, which was paired with a mismatched footstool.

Lawrence's bespectacled face showed the wear befitting a man past 85.

He often wore a bright blue, zipped-up jacket. His blue jeans had rolled cuffs, and he shifted his loafered feet.

"We had a coal stove in the basement," he said, pointing to the floor grate. I wondered aloud how anyone ever stayed warm in the unheated second floor when Al, Lawrence, and Eugene were kids.

"The three of us boys would sleep in a bed together to stay warm, on a straw mattress," he explained. "We'd pile on the quilts. You'd stay as snug as a bug in a rug."

Certainly, it was warmer than the day they received the news that sent chills down their backs. "When we heard about the accident, we were stunned; in shock for two weeks or more," Lawrence said. "You couldn't believe it. We got a phone call. 'Whattya mean?' You can't believe it."

The Bud Breitkreutz Band, 1936 or '37: Vernon "Bud" Breitkreutz, sax; Percy Krebs, drums; Eugene Schuld, accordion; Leonard Springer, violin, clarinet and sax; Ora White, piano; Percy Ihde of Jefferson, bass.

The wedding of Martha Pirkl and Leonard Springer, June 25, 1918. From left: Genevieve Packel, Frank Pirkl, Martha, Leonard, Alta Walker, Walter Springer.

The Musical Springer Family

"Mom says the first word she ever heard me say was a swear word."

"Dad would practice his fiddle in the barn. It drove the cattle nuts."

Dad, in this case, was Leonard Springer, who married Martha Pirkl, one of Johnny's sisters. Martha Springer bore two daughters; Helen in 1919, and Marjorie (or Margie) in 1926. By 1998, the eldest, Helen Josi, lived in a one-story apartment at Colonial Club Senior Activity Center on Sun Prairie's east side. When I visited her, she wove stories of music, happiness, and two wonderful parents.

"My Grandpa Charlie Springer played the fiddle at an old hotel in Madison," Helen said. "My dad learned to play the violin when he was propped up between two pillows. He was a wonderful player."

Her mother, too, was a musician. "Mom went to Watertown on a train to take piano lessons. Lots of kids did back then."

Helen learned to play the clarinet and the piano, but not under her father's tutelage. "He didn't have the patience to teach us kids. My mom taught us the piano."

Helen subbed for Ora White when Ora would get a cyst on his wrist, which prevented him from playing piano with the Bud Breitkreutz Band.

Helen showed me a photo of the band, taken in 1936 or 1937, she figured. Her father, the tallest of the performers, played violin, clarinet, and saxophone. Vernon, or "Bud," played sax, too. Percy Krebs played drums, Eugene Schuld the accordion, and Percy Ihde of Jefferson was "the greatest little bass player."

Sometime after the photo was taken, Ora fell from a roof and became paralyzed from the waist down. He had two ladders leaning against the house. He was stepping from one ladder to the other when the second one slid, and he fell, his back slamming into a pail of nails. At the time, Ora's three boys were ages five-14.

"Dad said we should have a big party for him because he wouldn't live long," Helen said. "But he outlived every one of the band members."

Ora indeed lived to a ripe old age. Records at Pederson Funeral Home of Waterloo state he died in 1992 at age 85.

At one time, five Springers played in the Marshall Band, a community group that, among other spots, performed after the harness races at the Dane County Fair. "Uncle Walter played the trombone. Dad played clarinet. Grandpa Charlie played trombone and, when he was too old, he played drums; Margie and I played clarinet and piano."

Before joining the Breitkreutz Band, Leonard Springer had his own orchestra, which Helen said was big in the 1920s and 1930s. "My dad had his own orchestra from about the time he was 17," she said, naming gigs in communities from Columbus to Monroe. She presumed that her Uncle Johnny Pirkl met his future wife through friends and believed that the couple danced to tunes played by her father's band.

She recalled joining the band for a trip in thick fog to the Jefferson County Fairgrounds. "We went through a gate and were driving around the racetrack," she said of the errant entrance. "People were standing on the pavilion porch, wondering who was driving around the racetrack."

The Medina Town Hall, across from St. Mary's, was a frequent performance spot. "At the town hall in Marshall, Dad played violin, and I played piano at a lot of functions. I can remember the town hall filled with blue smoke from cigars and pipes, so thick you could cut it. I still like the smell of a good cigar," Helen said, even though her husband, Leslie Josi, died of lung cancer.

While Leonard, Walter, Helen, and Margie followed Charlie Springer's musical lead, it was not with the blessings of Charlie's father, the conservative Charlie Springer Sr. When Charlie Jr. was performing at spots in Madison, his father told him, "You're going to hell for playing at dances."

Helen obviously grew up idolizing her parents, who were married in 1918. "My parents couldn't be beat. They were very popular, very well-liked, very handsome. "Mom was neat and clean. I can still see her up polishing the stovepipe. Mom had a beautiful garden, too. Dad was a wonderful carpenter. He built our house and barn. He was always helping others, too."

Her family's farm was on Canal Road near Marshall, just west of the intersection with Cherry Lane. The Springer farm sat on an east-facing hillside, protected from the westerly winds.

A Hellenbrand family owned the neighboring farm, closer to Marshall. Then, on another ridge, was the site of the Charlie Springer Sr. farm. When Helen was growing up, her grandparents, Charlie Springer Jr. and his wife, the former Agnes Packel, ran the farm with their son, Walter. When Walter got hitched, in his 40s, to Esther Callahan of Watertown, Charlie and Agnes moved to Waterloo.

Helen reminisced about a time in the late 1920s when a tornado whipped through. "There was straw driven into the siding on our house," she said. "Grandpa Springer walked down, picking his way through all the downed wires, to see that we were all right."

It's likely that Helen was recalling a tornado that ripped through Marshall in 1928. The book *A Nostalgic Look at Marshall*, compiled in 1976 for the community's bicentennial, shows a picture of a grain elevator sitting cockeyed after being hit by a tornado. The grain elevator was near the railroad depot, perhaps two miles southwest of the Springer farm.

I passed Helen a copy of a newspaper article that announced when Charles and Agnes Springer were to observe their 60th wedding anniversary with a dinner at their home in Waterloo. Their photo showed Charles, dapper in a three-piece suit, stark white hair cropped short, broad shoulders, and square features. His wife wore a printed dress and a modest grin. Her hair was slightly white around the edges.

Grandpa Charlie liked to make homemade wine, Helen remembered. "I'd pick currants for the wine. Sat on a milk bucket. I hated it at the time. I'd give a million bucks to do that now."

She recalled the time Grandpa Charlie was making dandelion wine in the basement and had a container brewing with a ring of raisins around the rim. Helen was maybe four years old, and she liked raisins. She reached up and picked off as many as she could, munching them down. Suddenly, she felt sick. Little Helen stumbled up the stairs, went outside, and fell against the windmill step, cutting her head. "I got sicker than a dog," she said, remembering vomiting; drunk, at about age four.

She thought back to the days when the men would play euchre, but instead of drinking alcohol, the table had a big bowl of greening apples. The fellas would curse as they'd bang a trump card on the table. The cursing left an impression on little Helen. "Mom says the first word she ever heard me say was a swear word."

Helen recalled colorful snippets from her Pirkl and Hady ancestors. "Mom remembered Grandma Hady smoking a small clay pipe at night, sitting with a little doily on her head.

"Frances Pirkl was laid out on the ironing board in the dining room at the Pirkl farm when she died," Helen said, referring to a common practice for a wake at a farmhouse.

Helen's mother, Martha, who somehow got the unusual middle name of Biana, told how her father would stick money in her shoe before she'd walk north from the Pirkl farm across the fields to the bank in Deansville.

The Springers emigrated from Germany, or Bohemia, or both, Helen said. The family settled in rural Waterloo, near St. Wenceslaus, or the "Island" Church, built in 1836, and now on the National Register of Historic Places. Eventually, the Springers wound up west of Marshall. Charlie Sr., Helen's great-grandfather, was born on a farm near Deansville, between Marshall and Sun Prairie. Later, he would work the land. I recognized the place as another Hellenbrand farm where, as a youngster, I often hunted pheasants with my sister's boyfriend, Randy Hellenbrand.

Charlie Sr. spent his later years in a house in Deansville. "He said it was too noisy in Marshall," Helen said, "so he retired in Deansville."

Helen's father was born in 1894. Walter arrived the next year. "Grandma Agnes said Walter followed Dad around like a little puppy. When Dad got the measles, Walter cried because he wanted to get the measles, too. Even in his later years, he couldn't seem to do anything without Dad along."

Helen had a photo of her parents. Leonard had straight black hair and stood about six-foot-two; Martha stood about five-foot-ten. "He was tall, dark, and handsome, with large eyes. Margie has his eyes. Mom was as beautiful as he was handsome. She was slender, had beautiful hair, and wore it in a bun. She didn't age at all. She looked 30 when she was 70."

Her parents weren't afraid of work. "They were hard workers; worked hard on the farm. Everybody did."

Martha Springer made great bread and baked kreplach, filled with prunes and apricots. She was a good seamstress, too. "We had beautiful clothes. You didn't have to be wealthy if you knew how to sew." Stitching, quilting, and satin provided fine trimming to the family's clothes. Beautiful hats featured wide brims. Leonard Springer wore spats—gray ones with black buttons—to keep his ankles warm in winter.

But the good times ended, the music stopped, in the summer of 1956. That's when Helen's father died of a heart attack at age 62. He'd been making hay at his father's farm. Helen was there, too, having picked strawberries to complement her mother's noon chicken dinner. Farmers, Helen explained, called their noon meal "dinner" and the evening meal "supper"; lunch was something served at school.

"Mother, that was the best dinner I ever had," Leonard said to his wife. Those were the last words he ever spoke to her.

"It's too windy to make hay," would be the last words he'd utter.

"He pulled the throttle out on the tractor, and over he went," Helen said. "The band played that night in Waterloo, so we had them take him to the funeral home. We thought that was pretty good."

Helen's mother died in March 1973, shortly after suffering a stroke, and just before her 79th birthday. She outlived her brother Johnny by more than 45 years.

A Grown Man Cries

"She was quite a popular girl."

Russell McCarthy, still handsome with his white hair, struggled to remember the former Hazel Ferguson. Tears ran down his cheeks, and he rolled his tongue around as he wrestled to form the few words he'd offer.

"She was quite a popular girl," he told me twice, maybe three times.

Russell grew up on Town Hall Road on a farm now owned by Keith and Joan Rademacher, situated south of the Pierceville Town Hall. Destiny would have him gripping Hazel's casket as one of his lovely, young neighbor's pallbearers.

"The Pierceville Women's Club sponsored a '500' card party each week. They had one at the Ferguson farm. That's how I knew Hazel."

Russell told me what he could remember of the Fergusons: Hazel's parents, John and Ida, and her Uncle Carl, who never married. "They were good neighbors, pretty well-off for those days. John Ferguson was very tall. Ida was a small woman. They didn't get married young; he was pretty well-off when they got married." After Johnny and Hazel's accident, "Her mother took it awfully hard. She never recovered."

Russell recalled the days when he would go with his brother and friends to Angell Park in Sun Prairie to dance.

"For a few years, I never missed a week going to those dances."

Did he recall how or where Johnny and Hazel met; at one of those dances, perhaps? He couldn't remember, but he offered, "When Hazel married Johnny, she left a couple of other guys on the sideline."

One was Clarence Blaschka, who "went with her awhile," but, alas, he got no closer than to serve as another pallbearer at her funeral. Russell remembered Hazel's other pallbearers, including his brother, Daniel, and neighbor Leonard Starker. "Leonard and I were exceptionally good friends. We traveled together a lot."

Russell and Daniel eventually bought a farm adjoining the Ferguson place. "I farmed all my life."

This summed up my visit with Russell McCarthy, age 90, pallbearer for Hazel Ferguson Pirkl more than 70 years earlier. Standing in the kitchen, his wife, Tess, said Russell's struggle to remember details didn't surprise her. His memory was fading, and he suffered from depression; the latter might be a result of the former, she guessed.

Later that day, I drove past the former McCarthy farm, which was adjacent to the Ferguson farm. It stood on the big curve of County TT, where the highway parallels Interstate 94. It dawned on me that my Uncle Fran and I had hunted pheasants on the property many years ago.

A sign west of the buildings read: "Future County Park Site, Russell and Ella McCarthy." I wondered who Ella was. A phone call to the McCarthy home a week later shed light on the situation. Ella McCarthy, Tess explained, was Russell's first wife. Russell married the former Ella Holt in 1939, and she died in November 1983. Russell and Ella were active in 4-H. He was a former Dane County Board supervisor, and then-Governor Gaylord Nelson appointed him to the State Board of Agriculture.

The couple's farm on Highway TT had a gravel pit run by Madison's Consolidated Paving Company. After the exhausted pit was filled in, the land was rented out and farmed for a while. Because Russell thought the county was spending too much for park land, he decided to donate the former gravel pit site for a youth park. Russell and Tess donated the 180 acres to the county in 1996.

Ruby "Tess" Hinze and Russell McCarthy met through mutual friends when he still lived on the farm and she lived in Madison. They wed in 1985, the year the McCarthy farmette—the buildings and 13 remaining acres—was sold to Victor and Janet Horstmeyer, whose son David now lived there.

Tess and the Dane County Register of Deeds office provided more background on the McCarthy brothers. Daniel was born in 1905 in Sun Prairie to New York native Thomas McCarthy and Mary Connor, who was born in Sun Prairie Township. Russell came along in 1907, at about the time the white farmhouse was built on Town Hall Road. Russell graduated from Sun Prairie High School in 1924.

I asked Tess, who was obviously younger than Russell, to reflect on his earlier years. "Russell was very active," she said. "He had a lot of pep; always a busy person. He liked people and had a very likeable personality. Everyone liked him."

Russell had told Tess that when he was five years old, his mother took the boys to the local bank and gave them each five dollars to open savings accounts. "That first lesson in saving stuck with him. They'd always put money in their bank accounts." Later, Russell played a role in starting Valley Bank.

Tess described Russell as sensitive, compassionate, and diplomatic. "He had a nice way of doing things. He didn't make people angry with him. He was patient and determined. He kept at it and did a job until it was done. He carried things through without riling a lot of people. When he believed in something, he'd fix a problem, do what he could to improve it."

A fun-loving person, Russell liked to tell clean jokes, Tess said. His brother, Daniel, was well-liked, too; friendly, and a hard worker.

"Russell was a lot smaller-framed; both worked hard, but Daniel would try to shoulder the heavy part. Russell was sickly when he was young. As a baby, his first year, they were not sure he was gonna live. Then they bought a goat when he was one, and the goat's milk helped him. When he was nine months old, his mother was peeling potatoes, and he reached for one. She told the doctor. The doctor said, 'Then give him some.' His health improved then."

Daniel died young, at age 37. The brothers bred cattle on their farm, and Daniel had driven to Iowa to deliver a bull. "There was bad weather," Tess explained. "He dozed off and got hit by a train, not far from home, about three miles."

The death certificate at the Register of Deeds Office filled in the blanks. The accident, July 16, 1942, in Sun Prairie Township left Daniel with skull, vertebrae, and rib fractures. He was buried in Sacred Hearts Cemetery, Sun Prairie, and left a widow, Isabel Almond, age 25.

Russell J. McCarthy died at age 91 on January 26, 1999, at University Hospital in Madison. A couple of months had passed before my father informed me of the death.

His obituary stated that he had farmed in Sun Prairie from 1925 to 1951. He was a lifelong member of the American Milking Shorthorn Society and won the Grand Champion award at the Minnesota State Fair in 1951. He was also a member of the Dairy Shrine Club. Russell served 25 years as a 4-H leader. He served on the State Board of Agriculture from 1960-1969 and on the Sun Prairie Town Board from 1960-1966.

A phone call to the Dane County Clerk's Office brought a copy of a resolution, a "Memorial to Russell J. McCarthy," signed February 4, 1999, and presented to the McCarthy family. It states that Russell served on the Dane County Board, representing Sun Prairie, Cottage Grove, and Blooming Grove townships, from 1966-1982. He served as chairman of the Highway Committee, vice-chairman of the Parks Commission and also on the Finance and City-County Liaison committees.

On the donation of 180 acres of land, it read, "where children from the city could learn about nature. A masterplan for this park has been drawn up and, with the help of funds also donated by Russell and Ella McCarthy, development will begin in 2002."

On September 29, 2002, the county, having acquired more acreage, organized a grand opening for the 220-acre McCarthy Youth and Conservation Park. It became Dane County's first park with horse trails. I stopped one day in 2003 while it was still in development. I found it ironic that on lands where farmers once toiled and tilled the fields behind plow horses, horse lovers could now traverse park trails for the sake of pleasure.

A Lone Link to the Fergusons

"Those days, it just wasn't done, changing religions to get married."

As the new millennium approached, Phoebe Bakken was the only known survivor on the Ferguson side of this story. Phoebe's great-grandmother, Elizabeth Bulman, and Hazel Ferguson's grandma, Louise Ferguson, were sisters from New York, Davis being their maiden name. That would make Hazel's father, John Ferguson, and Phoebe's father, George Bulman, cousins once-removed and Phoebe and Hazel shirttail cousins.

Phoebe was a wisp of a woman, a former schoolteacher, full of wit, and warmer in person than on the phone. Her gray hair and large glasses framed a hearty smile. She was living in a comfortable housing complex for the elderly in the newer section of Cottage Grove. Her second-floor apartment was attractively decorated with antique furnishings. Among her cherished trinkets, two were most intriguing.

One was a hand-blown vase, covered with a film of dust from months of sitting atop her kitchen cabinets. Phoebe was too tiny and too frail to climb up and clean that area. I reached up and removed the vase from its lofty location to inspect it more closely. It was green with white swirls; about three inches wide at the base and top and narrower in the middle. The top ridge was fluted, spread out in a melted look. This vase was a wedding gift for Johnny and Hazel from Phoebe's parents, George and Laura Bulman.

"It doesn't sound like much of a wedding gift now," Phoebe said. "But in those days, it was. I used it many years."

The other item was a tin salt and pepper shaker set. The shakers were hand-painted, green with tan tops and bottoms, and speckled with pink and yellow flowers. The matching tin stand was green, and the handle was twisted into a spiral. This item was Phoebe's shower gift to Hazel Ferguson. Phoebe was born June 22, 1921. She was six years old when Johnny and Hazel were married.

"Did you attend the shower?" I asked.

"No. You didn't go to many things in those days. It maybe was not a formal shower anyway; just a gift you gave before the wedding."

Phoebe thought for a moment about the bride.

"I remember Hazel as a pretty girl. Hazel looked like her mother. I didn't go to the wedding; not many did on our side because of the change of faith."

After Hazel died, her grieving mother, Ida, returned the shower gift to Phoebe.

Phoebe grew up on the hillside farm close to Gaston School. It was an easy walk to school, and she could go home for lunch. Phoebe's mother, Laura, had been a teacher at the school, but she never had her daughter in her class. Her courtship with George Bulman shortened her career—teachers weren't allowed to be married.

"That's how my dad met Mom," Phoebe said. "They always teased Dad that his cornrows went right toward the schoolhouse before they got married."

George and Laura Bulman were married in 1901. Besides Phoebe, they also raised a son, Neil, born in 1919. They raised Guernseys and tobacco. A photo of the homestead shows a dairy barn, a combination granary and tobacco strip house, a shed for drying tobacco, a chicken coop, woodshed, windmill, and the typical two-story farmhouse.

Phoebe's Grandpa Frank Bulman lived with them. With a grandfather and brother on the farm, Phoebe's main responsibility was tending garden: picking potato bugs off the plants and dropping them in a pail with a splash of kerosene in the bottom, digging potatoes, pulling radishes, and harvesting the assortment of vegetables. When her brother went into the service, Phoebe had to learn to drive the tractor.

Interstate 94 now dissects the former Bulman farm, which consists of a ranch home and a barn in need of paint.

Decades before the superhighway went in, Phoebe trudged a snowy path a mile or more to the John and Ida Ferguson farm to skate on Koshkonong Creek. She and Neil could stop at the Ferguson place to warm up.

"We'd walk up to the Ferguson farm and sit on the oven door to get warmed up after skating. We always stopped at the Fergusons. I can still see the oven stove, and those doors always held you. You were always made welcome. We'd drag snow in, and that didn't matter."

"Would Ida serve a snack?" I asked.

"We weren't the Norwegian type, where you'd stop in at those places and there'd be food."

Even Phoebe's schoolmates made use of the Ferguson farm. "We had school picnics in the woods by the pasture, by the creek. We'd walk in the driveway and out the back way."

Those were fun times. Phoebe believes the fun of a big family such as the Pirkls is what attracted Hazel—an only child—to Johnny.

"I think that was one of the things that intrigued her. Here was a family, a lot of activity, things going on. I think Ida had fun in her that Hazel had. At that age, a family like that is wonderful, very interesting. And Johnny probably thought Hazel was neat just by being by herself."

Thoughts of fun and happiness soon turned to reflections on anguish, heartache, and sorrow. Obviously, the wedding and accident changed the Ferguson family forever.

"For many years, it wasn't popular to talk about things that happened," Phoebe said.

The wedding had driven a stake through the family. John Ferguson was so upset about his daughter's wedding that he refused to attend it.

"They always said it was because he was against it. You feel like a stranger going to a Catholic ceremony. Not only didn't he think it was right, but he was uncomfortable about it."

Traces of racism surfaced in the 1920s. The Red Scare triggered a roundup of 100 suspected Communists who were placed in a Detroit impoundment. The scare also triggered 3,000 arrests nationwide and the deportation of political undesirables. Intolerance sparked ill feelings toward blacks and Jews, or toward any group that seemed foreign or "un-American." Many people were suspicious of Roman Catholics because of their allegiance to a foreign pope, and because many members chose to educate their children in church schools instead of placing them in public schools.

The combination of fear and hate fueled the rise to power of the Ku Klux Klan. Southern Wisconsin was not immune from the Klan's reach. Racists opposed the migration of blacks in search of jobs in northern states. Racists also objected to Jewish and Catholic immigrants.

Sentiments against Catholicism may well have spilled over into the Ferguson household, where John Ferguson vehemently opposed the Catholic wedding of his daughter to Johnny Pirkl. This is not to suggest that the Fergusons had any association with the KKK; yet, with mistrust of Catholics so pervasive in that era, it is possible that these misgivings affected John's attitude toward Johnny Pirkl.

"My grandfather wasn't into the formal church thing," Phoebe said. "He did most of his religion at home. And John Ferguson and my grandfather had the same background. Grandpa didn't get involved in the church. He didn't care if they built anything or who the pastor was. They were Christian, but they weren't the type that were going to trot off to church every Sunday. My dad did more because of my mother. I can still see him standing in church. He liked music but wasn't much of a singer."

Phoebe said her mother was a Methodist before becoming a Presbyterian. She was uncertain as to the religion of the Fergusons, but she thought they went to Marshall for church.

"Those days, it just wasn't done, changing religions to get married. Now, everybody accepts everybody else, or tries to. I think it was fear. You'd be losing your only daughter anyway, but then you'd be losing her to another religion, too. It probably wasn't all about religion; a lot of dads don't like who their daughters marry anyhow, whether it's religious or otherwise."

Phoebe Bulman, daughter of Frank and Laura Bulman, in her wagon, 1923.
Phoebe Bakken in 1998, right.

Born in 1902 in Dane County's York Township, Harold Freidel was slightly younger than Johnny. By 1997, Harold, at age 95, was one of Marshall's oldest citizens.

"We saw Johnny and Hazel at dances," he told me, as he sat in his room at a nursing home in Sun Prairie. "We met them there. They were good dance partners."

Harold remembered the feelings of Hazel's mom and dad regarding the marriage of Johnny and Hazel.

"Her mom said he'd rather see her dead than marry Catholic," Harold said of John Ferguson. "That was the word I heard."

Others had heard that John Ferguson supposedly proclaimed, over the caskets of Johnny and Hazel; that they'd rot in hell. Phoebe Bakken doubted such words.

"He wouldn't talk like that," she said, matter-of-factly. "If he thought it, he wouldn't say it. He was quiet. He might have been mad as hell, but he wouldn't say it."

Phoebe remembered John Ferguson as clean-shaven, of ordinary size, and humped.

"I don't think the Fergusons were very big. John sat around the kitchen, looked outside, looked at the newspapers, did the chores. Ida was busy but always happy that we'd stop. Ida acted a little childish, taking someone's glasses off, maybe remembering her daughter a bit, after the accident. Maybe she had Alzheimer's or hardening of the arteries."

Years later, the Fergusons sold the farm and moved to a smaller, 1½-story home in downtown Cottage Grove. Phoebe remembered stopping in, visiting, and shopping on Saturday nights.

"He was such a good person," Arlene Weichmann said of Hazel's Uncle Carl, who lived to age 98. "He was a nice, kind person. He enjoyed talking with you. You could sit down and have a conversation with him."

In a brief phone conversation in 1998, Arlene told of her few memories of Carl Ferguson, who died of probable pneumonia two weeks after breaking his hip and developing an infection in the wound. Arlene had worked more than 50 years at Herreman's, a restaurant on Main Street in Sun Prairie. Carl also worked there as a dishwasher and helper from about 1950 to 1955. At the time, he lived in a Main Street rooming house that now housed Prairie Flowers & Gifts.

"He was up there in years," Arlene said of her long-ago co-worker.

If Carl, born in 1874, was working there during those years, he celebrated his 80th birthday while an employee of the supper club.

Phoebe's apartment gave evidence of her years as a teacher. Items of historical interest were everywhere. A horizontal photograph, more than three feet long, showed a large threshing crew from the Dakotas. A twister later flattened the barn in the photo, Phoebe said.

She pulled out genealogical information showing that her mother's great-great-great-great-great-great-great-grandfather, John Wood, emigrated from Holland on a ship called the Hopewell in 1646. He landed in Massachusetts, and it took him two years to pay off the passage and become a "free man." Phoebe admitted that tracking the Bulman genealogy had been much more difficult than documenting the Wood family. She hoped that Sara Steele, well known for her genealogical research in Cottage Grove, would work on it again.

Genealogical information pertaining to the Bakkens, Bulmans, and Fergusons explained that Phoebe's great-grandparents, William and Elizabeth Davis Bulman, from Utica, N.Y., had two sons who settled in the Cottage Grove area. One was Frank G. Bulman, Phoebe's grandfather, who married Phoebe Stickles. He died in 1942 at about age 90 as a result of a fall.

Phoebe's father, George, was born in 1877 and married Laura Wood, the daughter of Manley Wood and Rosalina Brown. The Wood family came from Marshall; the Browns hailed from Jefferson. George died in 1959. His wife, younger by two years, died in 1968. Both lie at rest in the Cottage Grove Cemetery.

The information gathered from Phoebe and Sara Steele created some confusion. Apparently Phoebe Bakken did not know who Hazel's maternal grandparents were, and much of the recorded information was incorrect. For example, a record from the Bulmans indicated that John Ferguson's brother, Carl, died in 1872. Because he was born in 1874, this was an obvious typo error. He died in 1972, according to a microfilmed obituary in the Wisconsin State Journal. Also, the information from Sara on the year of death for Hazel—1923—was incorrect.

The most baffling misconception was the belief that Charles Schoen and Matilda Pauline Kluck were Ida Ferguson's parents and thus Hazel's maternal grandparents. That information was recorded on a typed list of family members found in Phoebe's records. Sara provided me with the same misinformation by phone.

The information was wrong because Schoen and Kluck were parents of an Ida M. Ferguson. Part of the problem stemmed from the fact that Ida M. died at Dane County Hospital in Verona, and Phoebe Bakken recalled visiting Hazel's mother there. I was guessing that Phoebe, her memory a bit faded, was mistaken.

The death certificate for Hazel's father, John Murry Ferguson, who died at age 69 on November 3, 1941, at St. Mary's Hospital in Madison, lists his wife as a patient at St. Mary's in Madison and other survivors as a brother, Carl, at home, and a sister, Mrs. L.J. Groat of Norvell, Michigan. The gravestone next to the Ferguson monument in the Cottage Grove

Cemetery lists his wife as Ida H., born in 1869.

I was further puzzled as to why the year of Ida H. Ferguson's death wasn't engraved on her gravestone. Was she not buried next to her husband?

Sara Steele finally turned up a piece to the puzzle in early 1998. She wrote me a letter after finding Hazel's birth certificate that listed her mother as Ida Akin. Yet Sara could find no marriage license or death certificate in Dane County for Ida H. But she did find a memorial card for her at the Sun Prairie Historical Society.

"I am very puzzled as to where she is buried," Sara wrote. "The Pierceville Cemetery has a stone for her with a date given. However, the memorial card said that she was to be buried at Cottage Grove. There is a place for her with John, but the death date was never filled in."

A later search of records at what had become Tuschen-Newcomer Funeral Home in Sun Prairie turned up another memorial card for Ida H. Ferguson. It gave the date of birth as October 30, 1869, and the date of death as June 7, 1950. Services were two days later, at 9 a.m. at Tuschen Funeral Home and 9:30 a.m. at Sacred Hearts, the Rev. Monsignor G.A. Haeusler officiating.

Another slip of paper listed cars in the funeral procession: 1. Mrs. Lois Bagley; 2. Sibyl Mitchell; 3. Pirkl-Walker; 4. Mrs. Harvey Thew. While names linked to three of the four cars failed to strike a chord, the names "Pirkl" and "Walker" verified that this, indeed, was Hazel's mother.

Still, the burial situation remained a puzzle. Was Ida H. Ferguson buried at Cottage Grove, Pierceville, or in a Catholic cemetery somewhere? The Tuschen-Newcomer Funeral Home suggested I call Gary Pechmann, caretaker for Cottage Grove Cemetery. After several frustrating months of playing phone tag, Gary told me he had no written record of Ida being buried next to John, even though a stone for her sits to the left of the Ferguson monument, with no date of death filled in. He also guessed that Ida was buried there because it is customary to bury a first spouse next to her husband. It's probable that, with so few immediate family members surviving at that time, no one paid to have the date of death chiseled into the stone. Gary said he could use a rod to probe the burial site because, in 1950, the casket would have been placed in a cement vault. If it's there, the rod would hit it.

The thought of this action was somewhat disturbing to me, but Gary said he was willing to check. Not surprising, we played more phone tag. Then, one morning in September, Gary left me a message: Ida Ferguson lies at rest behind the Ferguson monument.

While Ida's burial site was confirmed, where she resided at the time of death remained a mystery. The Wisconsin State Journal microfilm provided the answer. Ida's obituary was published Thursday, January 8, 1950, and said Ida Fergusen (sic) died Wednesday at the Dane County Hospital and Home, Verona. Services were at Sacred Hearts, and burial was in Cottage Grove village cemetery.

"Mrs. Fergusen spent most of her life in the Sun Prairie and Cottage Grove area. Her husband, John, died in 1941."

Besides the wrong spelling for "Ferguson," the next detail was troubling:

"A daughter, Hazel, died in 1930."

This piece of information was off by three years.

It listed survivors as a sister, Mrs. Lois Begley, Chicago; a half-sister, Mrs. Frank James of West Virginia; and a brother, Frank Aikens, Arizona. Again, "Begley" or "Bagley"? Carelessness with spelling explains why Hazel's birth certificate lists her mother's name as Ida "Akin" and why Ida's obituary lists Ida's brother's name as "Aikens."

I assumed that Lois Begley (Bagley) probably provided the information, and with family members in various states, Hazel's year of death was a guess. At least it provided the final residence, confirming that Hazel's mother, Ida H. Ferguson, just like a woman named Ida M. Ferguson, died at the Dane County Hospital and Home.

Phoebe Bakken's memories of visiting Hazel's mother at the hospital in Verona had served her well.

We Meet Again

"Johnny wouldn't recognize the place."

Johnny Pirkl would undoubtedly think he was lost; that he'd pulled his Chevy into the wrong driveway. He'd turn to his bride and give her a puzzled look if he drove into the black-topped driveway of Mark and Mary Munson's farm on Highway T. Johnny wouldn't recognize the place; not by looking at the buildings, hidden from view of highway traffic by a slight hill crest.

But if Johnny were to look beyond those buildings, he'd recognize the place where he and his siblings grew up. There would be no mistaking the huge hill to the west, even though it's now covered with a tangled mass of trees, bushes, and briars. Johnny would remember the marsh to the south, often too wet in spring for a team of horses to pull a plow through. And he'd remember the windmill that once provided fresh, cold water to the family's grazing Durham dairy herd in the heat of summer.

But the buildings would leave Johnny and Hazel Pirkl stunned. The cluster of structures looks more like an estate than a working farm. Gone now is the antiquated, mice-infested, cobbled-together farmhouse, its wood stove, well pump, and worn wooden floors. Gone, too, are the outhouse, the pigpen, the smokehouse, and the workshop.

Yes . . . the farmhouse. What a fine-looking building it is today! The beautiful two-story home is much larger than what Johnny would remember. It's the house Frank Pirkl built in about 1955 on the site of the original farmhouse. But even Frank wouldn't recognize this home. Mark Munson expanded it with a playroom and fireplace, and with a large, windowed addition on the back that overlooks an in-ground pool. Munson also raised the roof to add four bedrooms. Johnny wouldn't relate to the electric stove, the microwave oven, or the flush toilets.

The expansive home is nestled among other impressive buildings. Several that were constructed in the 1940s and 1950s—such as the machine shed and the pig barn—have been refurbished. A large barn with new, white aluminum siding has snappy green trim that matches the roof. Two other buildings are finished in cedar siding—a contemporary, upscale choice.

At almost every turn in my research, I was struck with connections and tie-ins between my family and the Pirkl family. It wasn't surprising then to learn that Mark and Mary Munson now own both the Pirkl farm and the Peck farm across Highway T.

In January 1998, a few months after my father sold the Peck farm to the Munsons, I visited Mark and Mary. Mark told me they bought the L-shaped Pirkl farm—about 155 acres—in 1991. The triangular parcel by the highway is owned by another party. Mark is a drywall contractor, and his construction knowledge paid off as is evidenced by the buildings that stood around us.

During our chat, Mark explained that he had graduated from Deerfield High School in 1975. He mentioned that his kids were active in sports in Marshall, and that he knew Jeff Heiman. It was ironic . . . Jeff and I were on the starting five in varsity basketball our senior year at Marshall, and we graduated together in 1975, I told him.

"Then we must have played basketball against each other," Mark said.

Mark Munson was a starting guard for Deerfield's team his senior year. I also played guard, so we squared off one-on-one on the basketball court twice that season.

I wanted to hike around the property, snap a few photographs, and get a better feel for the land. Mark welcomed my exploration.

Outfitted with hunting boots and camera, I trudged toward the marsh. I reached the old windmill, briars and farm junk littering its base. The windmill stood guard over the marsh, waiting to quench the thirst of a passing cow. But cattle may never come this way again.

I discovered a badly rusted wagon wheel propped against a tree where a small savanna of huge oak trees provided a leafless canopy of branches. I wondered if Johnny Pirkl had left the wagon wheel there. The wheel and windmill were two visible reminders of a bygone era of farming—when the Pirkls tilled the land, harvested the crops, and survived by their sweat and ingenuity. Now, no farm animals graze on these acres. Furthermore, Mark did not till an acre. He rented the land to John Blaska, who operated a large farm.

I headed back to the farmhouse, snapping pictures of the windmill and the many outbuildings. I took the plowed drive and headed toward the hill. There I found a snowmobile path that provided a compacted trail for my hike. I marveled at the beautiful farmland, covered mostly with corn stalk stubble jutting through winter's white blanket. I struggled because of the hill's steepness, fighting through briars and thorn bushes, crawling over fallen timber, and looping around hickory and oak trees. From the top of the hill—a deposit left by the last glacier to cover Wisconsin—I could see that the ridge stretched for over a mile.

I found a small clearing and recalled a story relayed by Mark, as told to him by his aging neighbor, Marvin Albrecht. Marvin said Indians once used the hill as a ceremonial site, and that the farm families would find arrowheads on the ridge. It was a landmark that Indians would have found easily, I imagined. Mark also told me he got a chill every time he crossed a certain spot on the hill crest; it was as if the spirits of Native Americans walked there. Suddenly I had a far-fetched thought. Did the spirit of Johnny Pirkl return to the land to walk with them?

Mark was at a ballgame with his children when I visited his place again in July 2000. But Mary was cordial and agreed to give me a tour of the various buildings. Many weeks had passed since John Blaska had planted a crop of soybeans. He also had planted corn on the adjacent Albrecht farm, and it had grown so tall that it obscured the view of the former Pirkl place from the Langer Road ridge.

The old pig barn had been re-done with new drywall and cedar siding. Mark stored his boat in the larger barn and his pickup and drywall tools in a garage. There was a large Morton building, white with green trim. Next to it stood an open-face building with new doors and old barn boards visible on the inside. The Munsons had moved the driveway back, Mary explained. The well pump and two pines stand where the dairy barn and milk house were once positioned.

One of Frank Pirkl's granddaughters had recently visited the farm, Mary said, and she noted the putting green where the horse barn once stood. Mark had burned down the old barn while Mary was giving birth to one of their children. Mark had done work for a golf course, and the operators, in turn, created this little luxury for him.

The garage next to the house had once served as the granary, Mary said. Other than the cement floor, the entire building looked new; fresh cement patched holes in the old floor. But in the original concrete, in the southeast corner, the initials M.P. remained visible; initials carved by Marian Pirkl, Frank's oldest daughter.

I told Dad he need not fret over the Peck farm. Mark's modus operandi was to refurbish lavishly.

But little had been done to it, Mary said. She was opposed to Mark putting as much time or money into it as had been done on the Pirkl farm. She said she liked the look of the old buildings. Mary's grown daughter and boyfriend were living on the Peck farm.

"They're happy with it the way it is," Mary told me.

The barn now housed sheep. The house had a new furnace. Maybe someday the carpeting would be torn up to reveal the hardwood floors below.

The Munsons also removed the old chicken coop, one of five buildings that stood on the Peck place when my father sold it. It had been moved to a farm on Box Elder Road. Mary had heard the story that the Peck family lived in the chicken coop after the fire in 1927 that destroyed the farmhouse; that it later had been moved to the Pirkl farm and may have been used for living quarters while Frank Pirkl built the new farmhouse in 1955.

But Dad told me she was mistaken. The Pecks lived in an old tarpaper brooder house behind the burned farmhouse until the new home was built on the original site.

"I tore it down," Dad told me by e-mail, asking if I remembered the event. My recollection was foggy. "The old outhouse sat there just a few feet away toward the road. Old Sears catalog for paper. Ma always tore the women's lingerie section out so as not to corrupt us boys."

On the former Pirkl property, Mark Munson had dug four ponds, a project guided by a state natural resources official. Mark pointed out a small hill, west of the house. It was the perfect spot for his children to sled and toboggan, and, indeed, those winter toys sat abandoned at the bottom of the slope. The Munsons had spread prairie grasses and colorful wildflower seeds on some of the acreage. It occurred to me they were returning the land to its original state, as it would have looked before the Pirkls disturbed it with their horses and plows.

It has been said that we do not own the land; we are only caretakers. We mold it for our particular use, and, eventually, we pass it on to succeeding families, who shape it to meet their needs. Here, the Pirkl and Peck families once carved out meager existences. Descendants sold the property to Mark and Mary Munson, who, in turn, brought forth their vision; a plan that included recreation, rental property, and minimal tillage. The land remains after its tenants pass on and turn to dust; dust, like the farmland—worked, used, and, often, spent.

III

A Twist of Faith

Dr. John Robert Curtis, historian and former veterinarian in Portage, poses near Bridal Pond.

Death Snatches Honeymooners

"The bridegroom's hand clutched the wheel of the automobile,
and his bride of a few hours had her arm around him."

"Death's hand interrupted a honeymoon here almost before the wedding bells had ceased to ring in the happy couple's ear," the *Capital Times* of Madison reported on September 29, 1927.

"With bridal bouquets on their breasts and old shoes dangling from their car, the bodies of Mr. and Mrs. John J. Pirkl of Marshall, Wis., were taken from the seven-foot depth of a pond in the Portage city park late yesterday. The bridegroom's hand clutched the wheel of his automobile, and his bride of a few hours had her arm around him."

That same day, a headline in the *Waterloo Courier* announced: "Marshall couple drowns in Wisconsin River while on wedding trip."

"Mr. and Mrs. John Pirkl drive over embankment at Portage," the first subhead read. "Married only a few hours," a second subhead stated. And, another: "Were to have begun housekeeping on farm bought from Fred Wakeman."

"Mr. and Mrs. John Pirkl, Marshall-Cottage Grove bride and groom who started on their wedding trip to Pine City, Minnesota, Tuesday following their wedding festivities at Marshall were drowned at Portage when their car went over an embankment into the Wisconsin River," the

Courier's story began, naming the river instead of the pond. "It was not until Wednesday that the disaster was discovered. State highway commission employees, following the unusual deep tracks off the main highway, discovered the car in the water. The bodies were removed from the car by Portage police, highway employees, and garage men at 3:45 p.m. that day. Identification was made from the spare tire casing on the back of the car, bearing the name of the Lazers garage, Marshall."

The story recapped the wedding scene, then, it continued:

"After sitting for wedding pictures at Sun Prairie, the newlyweds had departed at about four o'clock for Baraboo, where they expected to spend the first night. Relatives at home were happy in the belief that they were carrying out their plans until Wednesday when the Marshall marshal, Wilfred Radis, got the telephone call. The report was that after crossing the bridge over the Wisconsin River in Portage, the car had missed a turn in the road and had passed over an embankment. The dense fog of that evening probably was responsible for the tragedy.

"Mr. and Mrs. Pirkl, who had left their friends and family with so much anticipation Tuesday afternoon, had all arrangements made to begin housekeeping upon their return from the visit with the Ed Pirkl family at Pine City on the farm recently purchased from Fred Wakeman. They were to have been at home to friends after November 1. The entire community is deeply in sympathy with the bereaved families."

"Death Snatches Honeymooners," a page one headline stated in the *Portage Register-Democrat* on September 29, 1927.

"Death, in a most tragic and uncanny manner, interrupted a honeymoon here Tuesday at some unknown hour when a bride and groom, Mr. and Mrs. John J. Pirkl of Marshall, Wisconsin, plunged under eight feet of water in their new Chevrolet coach into a pond in the Portage city park.

"With a bridal corsage still pinned to the bride's dress, a rosebud still in the button hole of the groom's coat, and old shoes tied to their car, they were taken from the water late yesterday evening, having been discovered by O.H. Onsgard and G. Gilbertson, state highway commission employees. The car was submerged 24 hours before it was detected. These men had noticed the wayward tracks and had followed them to what they thought was an abandoned car but what proved to be the scene of a double tragedy.

"According to employees at the Wright Motor Company on DeWitt Street, the young couple had stopped there between the hour of six-thirty and fifteen minutes to seven and had inquired as to the road that they should take. They were a little undecided just which way they should go and discussed the question among themselves for a few minutes before leaving the garage. They evidently decided to go toward Baraboo and were headed in that direction on Highway 33 . . .

"The bridegroom's hands apparently had been clutching the steering wheel of his car as they were in that position when the body was pried from the car beneath the water. Both of the victims had received fractured skulls. This had evidently meant instantaneous death as neither showed any signs of having struggled for freedom after being pinned under the water. The windshield of the new car was broken and there was a huge dent in the back of the left side; outside of that and being water soaked, the car was practically undamaged.

"The bride's silver mesh bag, which contained a prayer book, a sacred heart badge, little vanity and three dollars and forty-five cents, was found hanging on the light of the dashboard of the car. The mesh bag, the suitcases, and other personal belongings of the couple were turned over to the Coroner C.W. Baker. The bodies were carried to Ingle's undertaking establishment."

The *Courier's* story contained at least one other factual error, which the *Capital Times* repeated. Johnny and Hazel had not crossed the Wisconsin River after their stop in Portage. They would have done so moments later had they correctly turned left instead of heading into the pond.

Other newspapers added snippets of detail. The September 29, 1927, edition of the *Milwaukee Journal* reported that the couple died within 12 hours of their wedding; that Johnny's body was found under the steering wheel; the bride was found on the seat beside him; and that, had they gone in one foot farther, they would have been in 16 feet of water instead of six feet, possibly making their discovery unlikely. Also reported was that they had driven through a clump of trees, and that Johnny's watch stopped at 6:30.

Contemporary newspaper stories add further details: the "Just Married" sign was still on the car when it was pulled from the pond; Lazers Motors verified the sale of the gray 1927 Chevrolet coach to John Pirkl when contacted about the identity of the two victims; and, all the wedding gifts were returned to their givers.

Veterinarian John Robert Curtis saw something in his Portage neighborhood at age 12 that would always stay etched in his mind.

"We heard about the car being in the pond," he said.

As a young boy, John hung out with a handful of neighborhood kids. Word of a car in the pond spread quickly! "In those days, you got a bike for your 10th birthday. Every place we went, we rode our bikes. So . . . we probably rode our bikes down to see it.

"By the time we'd gotten there, they'd already taken the people out of it. They had a rope on it, and 15 to 20 men got a hold of the rope and pulled the car out. Car wreckers were not numerous at that time. It was just as easy to get a bunch of men to pull it out. I remember the water running out of the car."

Interviews with friends and descendants shed further light on the tragedy and its effects on the family.

"Mom's idea of what happened is that Johnny hit the steering wheel and he had a concussion," Joann Ramseier said of her mother, Helen Pirkl, Johnny's sister-in-law. "Mom said Hazel had drowned; Johnny had a big bruise on his forehead. Everybody accepted the fact they both died immediately.

"Word has it that a county highway crew was working on the road and took the highway signs down. It got foggy and dark, and they went home. There was enough room for them to drive between two trees, and they went straight down."

"The city of Portage was so scared of a lawsuit because there weren't reflectors there that night," said Joann's sister, Marian Zimbric, recalling the story passed down by relatives. "They put them up the next day."

"There should have been signs up there," said Catherine Benesch, Johnny's niece, who was 10 at the time of the tragedy. "But in those years, people didn't travel as much. Grandpa said he could sue the city of Portage, but that wouldn't bring them back, so that was that."

Seventy years later, Dr. Curtis questioned the thought that all signage had been removed.

"Because of the type of corner it was, there had to be signs there," he said. But, he added, "I don't have the slightest idea if construction was under way."

The *Portage Register-Democrat* carried the story on September 29, 1927, but it cast more uncertainty with a sentence that would lead to speculation through the years: "Rumor has it that a flashlight sign had been placed at this crossing until a short time ago but had been removed."

Portage's city council met the next Tuesday, centering the evening's concerns on the water plant. But paragraph seven of the Page 1 story the next day, on October 5, shed some light: "The council argued the question of safety signs on water fronts and street ends, as well as general street and traffic safety conditions. Fifty signs were ordered by the city several weeks ago but have not arrived from the manufacturers yet."

That was it. The story offered no words of concern about the tragedy specifically; no comments on sorrow or regrets. The newspaper's account presented nothing to indicate whether the pond accident was mentioned in the discussion of inadequate signage.

Portage Daily Register columnist Dorothy McCarthy provided further details on the tragedy. One story appeared at the time of the new bridge in 1968; the other was carried in 1972.

"It was a miserable night. Heavy, thick fog rolled in off the river like a white blanket, reducing visibility to only a few feet."

The street workers noticed the erratic tracks in the muddy street the next afternoon. Cook Street was neither paved nor well populated in 1927. The street employees thought the car was abandoned, but "A horrified salvage crew discovered the couple still sitting upright in the front seat."

Seventy years later, three of Johnny Pirkl's nieces—Catherine Benesch, Helen Josi, and Bernadine Pirkl—visited the crash site. The three cousins posed for snapshots next to the Pauquette Park sign. The sunshine, lush greenery, and flowers made an idyllic setting for the photo. But behind the three ladies is the pond where Johnny and Hazel plunged to their deaths.

"They went between two willow trees," Helen said. "One is still there. If they'd have gone inches either way, they maybe would have died a different way."

Community of Sorrow

"The balcony was full at church the day of the funeral."

When the bodies of Johnny and Hazel were returned to Marshall, family friend Martha Langer, aunt of the best man, pitched in to help at the home of Joseph and Barbara Pirkl.

"Mom was there when they brought the bodies back to the house, and she talked about the clothes," said Martha's daughter, Patricia Kleinschmidt. "They took the clothes off and dried them as best they could. Hazel's father wanted to see her in her wedding dress; he felt so bad that he'd not gone to the wedding."

At least that was the story Patricia heard through the years; born in March 1927, she was a baby when the accident happened.

A story in the *Portage Register-Democrat* on Saturday, October 1, 1927, provided five paragraphs about the funeral:

"Residents of a sorrowing community will go to the St. Mary's church here at ten o'clock this morning following the call of funeral bells tolled to receive the bodies of Mr. and Mrs. John J. Pirkl, married Tuesday morning at the same church. . . . The same priest, the Rev. C.M. Nellen, who joined the couple in matrimony, will officiate at the last rites. Many of their wedding guests will sit in the same pews.

"Pacing solemnly down the aisle beside the flower bedecked caskets of the bride and groom will be more wedding guests of three days ago, a group of young men performing, as pallbearers, their last act of friendship for the dead couple . . . "

"In the same little church in which they were married three days ago, Mr. and Mrs. John Pirkl will receive Saturday morning the last rites of the Catholic church and will be taken to their final resting place on earth by some of the same companions who gaily showered them with rice and sent them on their fatal honeymoon last Tuesday," a *Wisconsin State Journal* story stated Friday, September 30, 1927. "Virtually every resident of this village will attend the double funeral . . . "

In its first issue of October 1927, a one-column headline in the *Marshall Record* stated "John and Hazel laid at rest."

The story backed into the tragedy, not mentioning how or where it happened until the fifth paragraph. Of the groom, it said, "John was a friend of all. His ready smile and good humor will be greatly missed by a large circle of friends. He was respected for his honesty, thoroughness and a strong determination to stand by the right . . . .

"Funeral services were held Saturday morning at ten o'clock at St. Mary's Church. They were laid to rest in a double grave in St. Mary's Cemetery at Marshall.

"The beautiful floral tributes offered and the host of relatives and friends from far and near, who attended the funeral, show in what esteem these young people were held."

The story continued: "Thus passed two young lives to their eternal rest. The gap which their going has left can never be filled on this earth. We can only hope to be with them again in the great beyond."

Following those words was a poem titled "There Is No Death":

"There is no death; the stars go down
To rise upon some fairer shore;
And bright in heaven's jeweled crown
They shine forever more.

"There is no death. The leaves fall,
The flowers may fade and pass away;

They only wait through wintry hours
The coming of the May.

"There is no death! An angel form
Walks o'er the earth with silent tread,
He bears our best loved things away;
And then we call them 'dead.'

"He leaves our hearts all desolate;
He plucks our fairest, sweetest flowers;
Transported into bliss, they now
Adorn immortal bowers.

"And when he sees a smile too bright
Or heart too pure for taint or vice,
He bears it to that world of light,
To dwell in paradise.

"And ever near us, though unseen,
The dear immortal spirits tread;
For all the boundless universe
Is life—there are no dead!"

A "card of thanks" followed:

"To the friends and neighbors who so kindly extended their sympathy
and assistance in our bereavement, to all who sent floral and spiritual bou-
quets, and to those who loaned their cars, we tender our sincerest thanks.

"Mr. and Mrs. John Ferguson.
"Mr. and Mrs. Joseph Pirkl and family."

Helen Josi, eight years old at the time, will never forget the smell of death at the wake at her Grandpa and Grandma Pirkl's house four days after Johnny and Hazel died.

"I still remember that smell coming from the caskets; pungent; a mix of pungent odor with the smell of flowers. Even Catherine Benesch said the flowers at the wedding made her sick. They showed open caskets at the wake and the funeral," Helen said.

Jim Langer and his family attended the wake at the Pirkl home. It was customary to have funeral visitations in the home back then, and this one was at the Pirkl house, the scene of much gaiety just days earlier. Hazel was dressed in her wedding gown, Johnny in his suit. Her flowers were still fresh, as was Johnny's boutonniere.

"The corpses were laid out; she had her veil and dress, and even the flowers she had were the bridal bouquet," Jim recalled.

During the funeral service at the church, as many mourners stood outside as were able to find seats inside in overflowing pews.

"The funeral was large," Jim Langer remembered. "The balcony was full at church the day of the funeral."

This time, Hazel's father entered the church. During the procession, John Ferguson walked behind the caskets containing the bodies of his only child and her new husband. But Hazel's mother, Ida, did not enter. She was too distraught.

Jim Langer remembered that John Ferguson's sister, Jennie Groat, was Catholic, and that she and John attended the funeral together.

"I can still see John Ferguson and his sister walking behind the Pirkls. I can remember she genuflected. Ida Ferguson had a heart ailment. She stayed in the car during the funeral."

"Hazel's mother was in such physical shock that she stayed in the car and had a nurse with her," said the former flower girl, Dorothy Voelker. "I think she grieved herself to death."

The October 1927 story in the *Marshall Record* listed the pallbearers: Daniel and Russell McCarthy, Leonard Starker, Clarence Blaschka, Darwin Bruns, and Malcom Adamson for Hazel; Walter Springer, Emil Langer, Paul Connors, Felix Lutz, William Hamshire, and the best man, Cyril Langer, for Johnny.

Sue (Catherine) Woerpel was the younger sister of William (Bill) Hamshire.

"I was surprised to see Hazel in her wedding dress, veil, and bouquet," Sue stated at age 83. "I was lucky enough to go along with the folks. We didn't stay long."

Walter Hamshire, Bill's younger brother, didn't attend. He had other plans. Walter was in high school in 1927, and J.O. Beadle, longtime principal and agriculture teacher, had obtained tickets for his male students to attend the University of Wisconsin's first game of the season. It wasn't hard to figure out why a wide-eyed high school student would pass up the solemn service for the excitement of gridiron battle.

"That was my first big football game I'd seen," said Walter, who couldn't recall the score or opponent. "That was something to see, and Wisconsin had quite a football team back then, too."

Bill Hamshire was born in 1902 and lived on a farm that adjoined the Ed Benesch and Walter Springer farms. Bill spent a couple of years at Medina Free High School, the former Marshall Academy, before farm duties called him home. Bill's friend Johnny Pirkl never went to high school.

"Johnny was a card, full of life," Walter recalled of his older brother's friend.

Walter Hamshire may have been too busy watching Wisconsin's 31-6 victory over Cornell to attend the double funeral. But his future wife, Catherine Feuling, who was 11 at the time, did attend the service. Catherine's family lived in Deansville.

"You knew everybody back then," Catherine reflected. "So it was no big deal to go to a funeral. We just went for curiosity because we heard it was going to be so big. We sat in back. It was so crowded, you couldn't see much."

Jim Langer recalled that Bill Hamshire and Johnny Pirkl performed together in "Lighthouse Nan."

"They probably went places together, dancing," Jim said of Johnny and his friend Bill.

Jim Langer also knew some of Hazel's pallbearers, who were mostly farmers. He knew, for instance, that the McCarthy brothers, Daniel and Russell, farmed near the Fergusons and were cousins of Paul Connors.

The scene was a bit different at St. Mary's Catholic Cemetery, a mile or two east of the church, on the outskirts of the village.

"The car with Mrs. Ferguson drove way up to the grave with the doctor tending to her," Jim Langer said. "They had to separate the people to get the car in there. Hazel's mom took one glance at the grave and looked back; she was so distraught.

"A lot of people came to the cemetery. Those days, everybody went to the cemetery, too. It was the first double funeral I'd ever seen. It was something that struck a real chord in the community."

The bodies were laid to rest in a double grave, one hole.

"It was over so fast," Dorothy Voelker said, "and they never came back—it was hard for me to understand that at the time. It makes you think about when somebody leaves, you might not see them again; when they go away, that emptiness; they may never return.

"I don't like goodbyes. Maybe that's why I'm such a worrywart."

Her brother Bob Walker added: "Our grandparents, what they went through, having the bodies in their home just after sending them off on their honeymoon two days earlier. Put yourself in their place."

"The tragedy was broadcast on radio nationwide," Dorothy Voelker said. "Memorials came from all over."

But the five-year-old flower girl and her younger brother Bob weren't among the mourners in attendance. The two kids stayed at the home of their Grandpa and Grandma Walker in Sun Prairie during the visitation, funeral, and burial.

"Mom said, 'I want you to remember them from the last day you saw them,'" Dorothy said. "That's probably the best thing my mom ever did for me; I didn't have to see the crying and the hurt."

Lawrence Johnson, neighbor and a cousin of the Pirkl clan, remembered vividly the scene one day when he was five, and he and his siblings, trudging back from school, crested that hill on the Pirkl farm.

"The car was sitting there on the grass by the windmill when we were coming home from school," he said of the 1927 Chevy that, just days earlier, became a tomb for his cousin Johnny and his wife.

Soon after, Jim Langer's family ventured to the scene of the accident.

"One month later, we went up to Portage, and the tire tracks were so deep in the mud they were still there."

Helen Josi would never forget when word came the day after the tragedy. Her little sister answered the telephone.

"When the call came the next evening, Margie picked up the phone and then called to Dad. Everybody was speechless. You just couldn't believe it.

"When you think about this young couple, they would have had a family, and it's so sad. Then some of these young people today who are throwing their lives away with drugs, and booze, and cigarettes.

"It's sad. It's just a rotten shame those two couldn't have a family that could carry on.

"Grandma Barbara and her sister Mary were in Watertown before she married, and a fortune teller told her that her youngest son would be killed. Fortune-telling was big in those days. After the accident, Mary asked Grandma if she remembered that forecast."

After Joseph Pirkl received money from Johnny's insurance company, he donated it to buy a stained glass window for St. Mary's; a memorial that filters late-day sunshine down on the altar.

At the home of Joseph and Barbara, a shrine of sorts occupied a corner bedroom upstairs for years after Johnny and Hazel deposited their belongings there before embarking on their honeymoon trip.

"Everything in the house was laid out just as they left it," Jim Benesch recalled. "We could look in the door, but we couldn't go in and mess around. That was sacred ground up there. That room was out of bounds, unless you got permission. And don't touch. And when Grandpa said, 'Don't touch,' you don't touch. The presents were sitting on the dresser and bed. The clothes were laid out neatly on the bed. I know it was like that quite a long time, maybe a couple of years."

A Brush with Death

"I can't believe that Grandpa could drive that car afterward."

No one who saw or heard about the accident would ever forget it. Not Johnny Pirkl's accident—but Joe Pirkl's accident—with the same 1927 Chevy that had carried newlyweds Johnny and Hazel to a watery grave.

After Johnny's accident, the car was returned to Lazers Motors to be cleaned and dried out. Then, Joe Pirkl, Johnny's father, drove the car for years.

"I can't believe that Grandpa could drive that car afterward," Marian Zimbric said. "But there must have been some feeling there. He wanted that car."

Marian's cousin, Dorothy Voelker, flower girl to Johnny and Hazel, had similar thoughts:

"Nobody could figure out how Grandpa could drive that car after the accident. It was the only car he ever had."

Marian's sister, Joann Ramseier, was among those who recalled Joe's accident with that same car. He was heading toward the Haefner farm, the former Wakeman place—the farmstead Johnny and Hazel intended to work. Joe had plans to paint the barn red.

"Grandpa bought a milk can full of paint. He headed over there in the car on a windy day, the paint can on the back seat. Mrs. Pautsch was on the phone," Joann said of the Pirkl family's neighbor. "She saw his car go off the road. The wind blew it off. She saw him crawl out all bloody. She thought he was a goner. It was all paint. They never got the red paint off the back seat."

Marian said, "Grandpa didn't get hurt. We brought him up to our house and got him cleaned up. The Pecks were the first on the scene."

Joe's grandson Jim Benesch added, "When Grandpa ran off the road, Bob Pautsch ran over there; thought he had his head cut off or something with all that red paint."

Marvin Albrecht reported, "He had red paint on top of his head. He had a red mustache then. It happened right by Pautsch's driveway. He never got hurt."

Lawrence Johnson, another neighbor and relative, remembered, "When Joe had the accident with Johnny's car, Bob Pautsch helped him tip it upright. Bob thought he looked like a clown, all covered with paint."

Dorothy's brother Bob Walker recalled how Joe generally took meticulous care of the car.

"Grandpa Pirkl always kept that car in perfect shape," Bob said. "I remember the gray-painted disc wheels. He'd hold a little paint brush up and spin the wheel and paint a red bead as a decoration on the wheels."

Joann recalled one other accident involving the car that happened when Joe and Barbara Pirkl were living in town, storing the car in an old barn, close to the walkway.

"Grandpa was driving one day when they arrived home in Marshall, and Grandma got out to open the door. But when she did so, Grandpa's foot slipped off the brake. The car lurched forward and pinned Grandma between the bumper and the door. It left her with a knee injury that she took to the grave."

When Joe Pirkl died in 1944, the family didn't keep the car.

"I think the car was sold back to Lazers garage," Marian said. "Some young boys in Marshall bought it and were driving it around."

Ron Wollin, a hired hand at the Pirkl farm when Joe died, remembered that two high school kids bought the car.

"I know it didn't last very long after they got it," Wollin said. "They wanted speed, and that car wasn't made for speed."

Jim Benesch said the family name was Spencer: George Spencer had two sons, Gordon and his younger brother, Russell.

"Russell Spencer got that car, I believe, and ran it hard," Jim said. "The family moved to California. That kid was kind of wild. God only knows what happened to that car."

Armstrong's clay pit for cream brick can be seen in the left half of this photo of early Portage from the last half of the 19th century.

Portage: Then and Now

"I don't recall the last time I heard somebody call it Bridal Pond."

Portage historian Ina Curtis, late aunt of veterinarian John Robert Curtis, summarized the life of Pierre Pauquette in her 1974 book *Early Days at the Fox-Wisconsin Portage.*

Fur traders made Portage the third-oldest settlement in the state—only Green Bay and Prairie du Chien pre-date it. In 1824, John Jacob Astor's American Fur Company sent Pauquette from Prairie du Chien to manage the trading post on the Fox River's east end. His father was French and his mother was a Winnebago, so Pauquette could serve as an interpreter between the Indians and white settlers.

Pauquette was renowned for his physical strength. One story told of how he helped pull a wagon across the portage between the two rivers when an ox failed to meet the challenge.

When troops built Fort Winnebago in 1828, in the region now known as Portage, Pauquette continued to trade furs. In 1836, the federal government called a council with the Winnebago, trying to get the tribe to sell land. Governor Henry Dodge suggested Pauquette may have been influencing the Indians not to sell, and with Pauquette being half-Indian, that may have been true. After weeks of discussions, no deal was struck.

In celebration, Pauquette apparently drank too much wine and, on his return trip to the ferry, he got in a dispute with an Indian named Iron

Walker near the site of St. Mary's Catholic Church. He slapped the Indian, knocking him down. Iron Walker got up, shot, and killed Pauquette.

A story titled "Old, New Lights on Pierre Pauquette," by Dorothy McCarthy, printed in the *Portage Daily Register* a couple decades ago, adds more detail.

On that fateful evening in 1836, Pauquette came upon the campfire of Man-za-mon-e-ka and his aging mother. They thought Pauquette was guilty of duplicity in the council negotiations and confronted him as he approached. After slapping and knocking down the Indian, Pauquette apparently kicked their campfire in disgust. It was then that the Indian raised his gun to fire. Pauquette calmly bared his chest and stated, "Shoot and watch a brave man die."

The Indian fired, and Pauquette fell dead at age 41. The Indian was tried and sentenced to hang. But the order was stayed, and he later was released. Still, he never dared to be seen in the Indian nation again because many tribesmen were determined to take matters into their own hands; they felt they had lost their most valuable friend.

Ironically, on July 10, 1927, just 2½ months before the Bridal Pond tragedy, the site had been declared "a dangerous nuisance." A committee was formed to plan for cleaning out the area known as the "old clay hole," incorporating it into a park, as originally intended, according to a 1968 McCarthy story in the *Daily Register*.

William Armstrong had established a brickyard at the site in 1847. The same site had produced the brick for parts of Fort Winnebago in 1828. The site included Armstrong's source of clay and his kiln. "Cream brick" was the primary construction material for commercial buildings, churches, and homes in the Portage region from the 1850s through the first two decades of the twentieth century.

Large deposits of white clay existed in pockets no deeper than three feet below a red surface clay in the Portage area. Significant calcium and magnesium in these clays produced the cream color of the brick. Portage had four brickyards that produced enough brick to supply local builders as well as users elsewhere in Wisconsin and Minnesota.

Armstrong's yard employed five workers in 1860. The business grew, and, by 1870, Armstrong produced 600,000 bricks annually. But by 1890,

Bridal Pond at Pauquette Park in Portage, 1950: A serene, picturesque place with a tragic past, where Johnny and Hazel's car slipped between two willows enroute to a watery grave.

Johnny and Hazel Pirkl may have seen St. Mary's Catholic Church as they passed it on Cook Street, on their way toward the pond at the curve in the road.

209

his brickyard had closed, leaving historic homes of cream brick to inter-
mingle with wood frame homes on both sides of Cook Street; and it left a
dangerous hole at the west end of the road.

The city bought the park property from Charles Hall for $1,500 in
1923.

A century after clay was dug from the spot for brick-making, work
began in earnest on the park reclamation project, which included cleaning
the pond and cutting excess vegetation and trees.

In January 1928, just four months after Johnny and Hazel died, the
park board sponsored a contest to name the park. The winner was to
receive ten dollars. Among the more than 120 entries: Armstrong, Zona
Gale, Ft. Winnebago, Sunset Tragedy, Honeymoon, and Bridal. Mary
Prescott, great-granddaughter of Pierre Pauquette, provided the winning
entry, Pauquette Park, though the park board apparently didn't realize she
was a descendant of the famous fur trader. Prescott later donated the prize
money to the Daughters of the American Revolution to help buy a granite
boulder and bronze marker at the site of Pauquette's ferry landing.

"Pauquette Park is looking its best now and is most inviting to visitors,
who are taking advantage of its beauty for pictures and walks," the *Register-
Democrat* reported June 12, 1928.

That same summer, three women's clubs—the Study Club, and the
Senior and Junior Golden Gossips—agreed to share the cost of the stone
wall and archway, which functioned as an ornamental gateway to the park's
east entrance. It also provided a measure of safety to motorists.

As keepers of historical records, Columbia County and Portage proved
to be most lax in regard to the tragedy of Johnny and Hazel. While the historical society has McCarthy's accounts, it did not compile the stories
relating to the Pirkls' calamitous event. The *Daily Register* had no clip file
related specifically to the Bridal Pond accident.

The Columbia County Register of Deeds Office should have death
certificates for Johnny and Hazel Pirkl, documents that might indicate if
the couple died of skull fractures, broken necks, or drowning. A book at the
Register of Deeds chronologically lists a handful of deaths for years of that
era, but there was only one entry for 1927, and it was neither Johnny's nor

Roger's Gifts & Gallery is now housed in the building where Wright Motor Company operated in 1927.

Wright Motor Company operated at 205 DeWitt Street in downtown Portage. Attendants at the service station were the last people to see newlyweds Johnny and Hazel Pirkl alive.

Hazel's. Seven decades later, a clerk surmised that the county failed, for some reason, to file the death certificates.

The coroner's office had no further information. By 1998, Coroner C. Keith Epps had held his office for about ten years and was certain no such record existed for the year 1927.

"Columbia County kept very poor records back then," he said.

Likewise, the Portage Police Department had no records dating from that time.

Roger's Gifts and Gallery sits along Highway 51 in downtown Portage. The building formerly housed an A&P grocery store. And before that, it housed Wright Motor Company, the Ford dealership where Johnny and Hazel stopped for gas on that foggy September evening.

If you drove past Roger's Gifts today and turned left on to Cook Street, you would see a senior apartment complex on the southwest corner. That spot once was known as "bank corner" because the First National Bank was located there.

Continuing on Cook Street, you'd climb the gently sloping hill and pass the tall steeple of St. Mary's Church. Stately historic homes—many made of cream brick—line the street, and then the road descends toward Pauquette Park. There, a stone wall—with an arching wood entryway and picket fence gate—stands as a barricade to any car that might skid off the road, toward the pond.

Westbound traffic on Highway 33 crosses the Wisconsin River on an expansive bridge. A visitor stopping at the park would turn right on Pierce Street before crossing the bridge; then left on Conant Street, and would end up in the park's small parking lot.

Plan a picnic for the park. Lounge on the grassy slope between the building and the pond. Marvel at the lone weeping willow tree. At the water's edge, you will notice a sprawling, flat stump of another tree, perhaps another willow that once stood about ten feet from the first. If it's May, a spring breeze may blow buds from the sweeping, lonely willow, some dropping in the pond, others landing in your face.

If trees could talk, would this weeping willow tell a sad story? Actually, that willow likely wasn't there in 1927. Weeping willows grow quickly, and they typically live only 20 or 30 years. A 1950 photo from the Portage Public Library shows the stone wall with two trees behind it. The one on the left is much larger than the one on the right, and its trunk looks different than the willow standing there today. The two trees pictured in 1950 are likely the ones Johnny and Hazel drove between 23 years earlier.

But were they willows? Perhaps. Forester Mary Ann Buenzow of the DNR office in Janesville examined a copy of the 1950 photo and said they could be ash or box elder trees. Yet the leaning tree trunks, type of bark, and the many shoots on the larger trunk are indicative of the willow tree. The leaves may not be fully developed, making identification a bit tricky. The library has no record of the time of year the photo was taken. It's unlikely anyone examining the photo would rule out the possibility that they indeed are willows, Buenzow said. Furthermore, she suggested, the willow standing on the edge of the pond today could have grown from a shoot of the tree that stood there in 1927.

Stroll along the south bank of the pond and up the levee that separates the pond from the Wisconsin River. At the top of the levee stands a marker telling the story of Pierre Pauquette and his ferryboat in the days before the bridge. Behind a glass-enclosed sign, you'll see pictures of the wooden bridge, built in 1857; its wreckage in the aftermath of a 1905 tornado; and the steel bridge built in 1906—the one Johnny and Hazel intended to cross; and the current bridge, completed in 1968.

In the middle of the display is a copy of the *Daily Register* photo and article, published June 19, 1996, telling the tragic story behind Bridal Pond's beauty.

On a lovely May day, a strapping young city worker is resealing the wood of a gazebo adjacent to Bridal Pond. He is a native of Portage. He is asked, "Have you heard of the Bridal Pond tragedy?"

"Oh yes. That's why they put that stone wall there, to prevent another car from plunging into it."

But a car had skidded off the road the previous winter, nearly winding up in the frozen pond used by ice skaters. That prompted a retelling of the Bridal Pond tragedy in the daily paper.

Another near tragedy occurred November 9, 2000. The lead story in the next day's *Portage Daily Register* described how a Ho Chunk tribal native drove his pickup into the pond at about 2:45 a.m. A passing motorist discovered the mostly submerged truck at about 7:20 a.m. Portage firefighters responded. The driver, when located, told police that he had fallen asleep, missed the curve, and plunged into the water. He had taken a taxi home.

Portage police officer Duane Pixler said the man was "pretty lucky" to have escaped. "That corner is a little different," Pixler told the *Daily Register*. "We've had houses hit, and now cars in the water."

The comment seemed to suggest that Pixler knew nothing of Bridal Pond's tragic history. Indeed, few people in Portage even refer to the hole as Bridal Pond. "They refer to it as the pond at Pauquette Park," said Curtis, the veterinarian. "In fact, I don't recall the last time I heard somebody call it 'Bridal Pond.'"

It seems that many Portage residents have forgotten, or never heard of, that tragic incident.

The First Daughter of Portage

"Keep it safe for the future."

It is doubtful that any one person has had a greater impact on Portage and its history than author Zona Gale. She played a key role in keeping the story of death in Bridal Pond alive by immortalizing the event in a short story bearing the same name. Gale wove a fictional tale of a man, Jen Jevins, who desired to kill his wife of 30-plus years. He slept with a gun under his pillow for a week, hoping to muster the courage to shoot her. Later, in a courtroom, he explained to the judge that he saved a boy from drowning in an old clay hole off the end of their property; that he took his wife for a nighttime stroll one foggy evening, and that he planned to push her into the pond where the boy had fallen in. Just then, a car, loaded with laughing occupants, missed the turn in the road. Before it plunged into the pond, Jens saw himself behind the wheel, in his wedding attire, with his wife, Agna, seated beside him.

Those in the courtroom rushed to the pond and learned that highway crewmen had discovered a submerged car, with only the top visible. To their horror, inside was a newlywed couple from Sun Prairie. An old shoe and "Just Married" signs were dangling from the vehicle.

Gale's story, published by Alfred A. Knopf in 1930 and reprinted in 1943 by her late husband, concludes: "The legend grew that Jens Jevins had had a vision of that happening of the night, and that it had sent him off his head."

Born in 1874, Gale became a poet, journalist, novelist, peace activist, civil and minority rights advocate, political progressive, University of Wisconsin regent, and supporter of the arts. The community celebrates her August 26 birthday on the third Saturday in August each year.

For years, Blanche Murtagh has spearheaded the annual "Friendship Village" celebration in commemoration of Gale's birthday. Veterinarian John Robert Curtis referred to Blanche as an "activist" historian, intending no ill by this description.

But one acquaintance warned: "Don't let her get started on the Portage Canal," the restoration of which she strongly supported as a historic landmark. Another said: "Don't get her started on the issue of sidewalks."

Blanche, a petite woman with a friendly smile and excitable nature—at least when it comes to causes, research, and history—could probably talk all night on Zona Gale. Eyeing her visitor's shirt from Kona, Hawaii, she noted, "I could squint a certain way and make that word look like Zona."

Blanche attempts to give the Gale celebration a new twist each year. In 1999, she considered an approach relating to Gale being a pacifist. "Wouldn't that be something, on a year like this," she said, as U.S. bombs rained down over Kosovo, and the new millennium drew near.

Small cities, Blanche said, are known for their cultural voids. "What the heck, a rod, a gun, a beer—culture," she said facetiously.

Blanche recalled another favorite quote: "People live their lives like there's going to be an encore. Do it nowwww! The day's the thing; the hour's the thing."

Born in Portage, Gale was an only child, raised with sensitivity and love within the intellectual and social confines of a small community. This information was from a Portage Landmark Preservation Society brochure; a project directed by Blanche Murtagh.

From 1903 to 1910, Gale wrote and sold 83 stories about life in small-town America, subtly veiling Portage people and places by calling it "Friendship Village." By 1914, nearly every book she published reached the bestseller list.

After her first novel, *Romance Island*, was published in 1906, Gale built a home in Portage at 506 W. Edgewater Street for her parents. Two front pillars make the "Greek Revival" home striking. It now houses the Women's Civic League, which Gale founded. Edgewater Street, at one time, was known as Canal Street until the "First Daughter of Portage" convinced the city fathers that the name wasn't attractive. After a stint in New York, Gale returned to Portage and lived in the Edgewater home and continued her writings.

"I'd see her going for walks," Curtis said of his childhood days. "She did a lot of writing in that house."

In 1920, Gale's novel, *Miss Lulu Bett*, shared bestseller honors with Sinclair Lewis' *Main Street*. When Gale adapted her novel into a play, it won the 1921 Pulitzer Prize for drama.

Gale died of pneumonia in Chicago on December 27, 1938, at age 64. She is buried in Silver Lake Cemetery, Portage.

Gale's life has one more connection to Bridal Pond. Gale enlisted the help of John Nolen, internationally acclaimed urban and parks planner, to create a vision for Portage's parks, including Pauquette Park.

Judge Howard Latton and his family have lived between the pond, the bridge, and the levee for more than 50 years. Blanche convinced him to write *Zona Gale: In My Back Yard* to explain how Gale and Nolen influenced the park's development.

In his 1997 account, Latton noted that during her time in New York, Gale obviously became acquainted with Nolen, a pioneer of the idea of public participation in planning. Most of Nolen's work was in cities larger than Portage. Some of the cities that he worked with include: Little Rock, Arkansas; Madison and La Crosse, Wisconsin; Columbus, Georgia; and Sarasota, Florida. Nolen apparently first visited Portage in 1908, consulting with Gale on town improvements.

Nolen probably saw the former Armstrong clay pit and area families driving their cows across the bridge to pasture each morning and evening. He prepared planting plans for private places in Portage and instructed the city on improvement projects, according to Barbara Jo Long in her 1978 thesis.

Nolen returned to Portage in 1910 to draw plans for Pauquette Park, according to a story in the *Register-Democrat* on November 12, 1934. He may have returned a few years later because, he writes in a 1913 letter to Gale, "I want to see what progress has been made."

In 1924, Gale accepted a position on the Parks Board. "So she contributed not only in attracting Nolen to lend his talents to the design, but she also helped administer the park," Judge Latton wrote.

A story in the Portage paper in 1934 announced Nolen's plans to revisit the city. Nolan raved about Portage's streets, which were curved to follow the river instead of being laid out in the traditional checkerboard pattern, common to most industrial cities. He also noted the many elms trees, mentioning the fact that they live longer than the maples that typically line city streets.

"The industrial cities, with their straight, treeless streets, know nothing of such beauty as the small towns have," Nolen told the newspaper. "Portage is a fine example of small town planning. Keep it safe for the future."

The 1996 *Daily Register* story—the one on the sign atop the levee—credits Nolen for his role in keeping the pond at Pauquette Park safe for the future: The Parks Board enlisted Nolen "to not only make the park beautiful but to make sure the newlyweds would be the last to drive to their deaths there. Nolen redirected the streets leading up to the pond and created the now familiar arched gate as a pedestrian access."

Catholic Conversion

"Ida was well into her 70s when she was baptized Catholic."

Before Jim Langer died, November 28, 2000, the former school principal offered one last piece of information that generated days of work to find corroborating evidence.

"The Fergusons later joined the Catholic church," Jim said. Then he added that he believed they became members of St. Patrick's Catholic Church in Cottage Grove.

Again, the irony: Hazel's parents originally were in strong opposition to their daughter's mixed-faith marriage and refused to attend the ceremony. Only Jim Langer, an observant teenager, was aware of Mrs. Ferguson's arrival at the church as the marriage service began, and her departure as it ended. Most surprisingly, the couple later joined the church they had once so disdained.

"I learned that through the Pirkls," Jim emphasized. "She joined first. They definitely became Catholic—that's as plain as the nose on my face."

The search for the religious origins of the Ferguson family took many twists and turns. The problem stemmed from conflicting stories told by various people.

The Fergusons were Presbyterians from Uttica, N.Y., speculated Marian Zimbric, niece of the late Johnny Pirkl. "They became Methodists because not many Presbyterians were around here."

In 1846, Cottage Grove had a Presbyterian church, said Phoebe Bakken, shirttail cousin of Hazel Ferguson. "But the Fergusons went more the Marshall way."

"Hazel's parents went to a Lutheran church in Cottage Grove, I believe," said flower girl Dorothy Voelker.

Helen Josi believed the Fergusons were Methodist. "We used to visit Hazel's parents, even when Johnny and Hazel were dating," said Josi, another of Johnny's nieces.

"Ferguson is a Scottish name, so it's likely they'd go Presbyterian," said Sara Steele, Cottage Grove genealogist.

Pierceville lies between Cottage Grove and Marshall, and the township had a church in the 1800s. Learning its denomination might be the key to determining the faith of the Fergusons. Where was it located, and what became of it?

Marshall mill-operator Ernie Blaschka heard that it stood on a diamond-shaped piece of property where Fred Mick's house was located, about halfway between the former Pirkl and Ferguson farms. A phone call to Fred Mick was in order.

Mick said the church once stood on his property. It may have been moved to someone's farm in the area. He was not aware of existing historical records or photos, but he suggested contacting his neighbor on Pierceville Road, Anita Henke.

Mrs. Henke was stumped. She suggested calling Albert Riege, who also lived on Pierceville Road. It seemed like a wild goose chase, but it was certainly worth another phone call. Albert's response: "The church is on my farm."

Unfortunately, the building was a disappointment. Riege used it as a granary. It sat behind the farmhouse, surrounded by other buildings. It had sliding doors and board siding, typical of farm buildings. A metal roof covered the 30-foot-by-40-foot structure. Inside were beams, grain stalls, and tools. The plank flooring sat off the ground on a fieldstone base. A brief examination uncovered not a hint of it ever serving as a church. But Albert wove a colorful story about how the building came to be on his farm.

"My dad, Paul, moved it to our place in 1921 or 1923. Dad and another man took all the planks off it and were going to move the frame, using a couple of wagons and horses. Just as they were gonna lift it onto the wagons, a big storm blew up, knocked the frame right together. The horses ran away and smashed up the wagons. So then they tore apart the rest of the frame and rebuilt it all."

Albert and his wife, Grace, offered valuable pieces of information on the story of the Fergusons and Pirkls. Grace joined the conversation, toting an old scrapbook chock-full of crumbling pages of yellowing newspaper clippings, which shed historical perspective on local businesses. Others told of weddings, anniversaries, and deaths—natural and tragic—and gave details on the Langers, Benesches, Walkers, Springers, and Pirkls.

Perhaps most valuable were obituaries for Johnny's parents, Joseph and Barbara Pirkl.

Because more than one person indicated the Fergusons may have been Presbyterian, a call to Pastor John Zingaro of Cottage Grove's Bryn Mawr Presbyterian Church was in order. He confirmed that Pierceville had a Presbyterian church, and that the Fergusons' names might be found on historical information compiled for Bryn Mawr's centennial celebration. He suggested calling Fritz Voelker of Monona.

Fritz indeed had the information on microfilm. On a page titled "chronological roll," was the name Hazel Fergison (sic) with the date March 21, 1920. She was at number 121, between Berdine (Graves) Stickel and Ray Lemon. The date was under a column called "received by" with a subcategory of examination month, day, and year. The next column was headed "If baptized on reception, indicate it here." In Hazel's line was written the word "yes."

A careful scanning of the rest of the microfilm turned up no more mention of the Ferguson family; not even among the donors for the new Presbyterian church built in 1896 for $845.

Several other entries were worth noting. Frank Bulman, Phoebe Bakken's grandfather, gave six dollars toward the construction project. Frank's wife was listed as a charter member. The date was September 17, 1900. Recall that the Bakkens were related to the Fergusons.

Phoebe's father, George Frank Bulman, was baptized as an adult on

March 22, 1902. He and his wife, Laura, were named to the roll of communicants with a certification date of March 30, 1903.

Phoebe Rosaline Bulman, No. 274, was baptized on reception on March 26, 1937.

Confirmation that at least one of Hazel Ferguson's parents turned Catholic came almost by accident in February 1999.

Sharon Quimette—pronounced We-met—of Sacred Hearts of Jesus & Mary Catholic Church in Sun Prairie had found and printed out a death list from the Sun Prairie historical library and museum that listed Ida, Hazel, and Carl Ferguson, but not John.

Sacred Hearts also has a record book that lists Ida Ferguson's funeral in 1950. Asked to look for more information about Ida and her husband, Sharon found a baptismal entry for Ida on January 12, 1943.

"That means Ida was well into her 70s when she was baptized Catholic," Sharon said.

The baptismal details listed Ida's birth date as October 30, 1869—a match for Hazel's mother. The priest who baptized her was G.A. Haeusler; the priest who would also perform her funeral seven years later.

Sharon said the baptismal details used the Latin words "neo/conversa," and she believed that meant Ida had converted to Catholicism the same day she was baptized. Because Ida's husband, John, died in 1941, it was not surprising that Sacred Hearts had no records for him.

The details also named a sponsor, Frances Blaschka. Also listed as Ida's parents were Morgan Ferguson and Martha White.

Obviously, unless her mother was indeed Martha and married a man named Morgan Ferguson, these individuals were not her parents.

The discovery of Ida's baptismal details led to another discussion with Pastor Zingaro; one that touched on the history of the Pierceville church, the 1920 baptism of 14-year-old Hazel Ferguson, and her family's apparent feelings about churchgoing and Catholicism.

As a young teen, Hazel likely spent a year or two in confirmation classes. On March 21, 1920, she made a profession of faith to become a member of the Presbyterian church; she could not have taken Holy Communion before that. She apparently was baptized the day she made her statement of faith.

Zingaro was puzzled that there was no mention of Hazel's parents in the records. "It's pretty odd that the parents wouldn't show up on Bryn Mawr records if she's listed on them," he said. Still, they must have considered themselves Presbyterians because it's "almost impossible to think she'd leave her parents' church to pick her own church as a teenager.

"Unless her parents were nonchurchgoers at all—that's one possibility. Maybe her parents didn't object to her going to church. It would be unusual for a teenager to join whose parents weren't already members. My guess is her parents were Protestants, and they themselves had that tradition and maybe heard some mean things about Catholics and never went so far as to join a church.

"People who farmed were working seven days a week, getting up at 5:30 in the morning or so. Maybe they never bothered to join, and maybe she (Hazel) had friends who joined, so they let her do that."

Zingaro speculated that maybe, after their only daughter's death, the couple sought consolation in the church. "Maybe in looking for a religion, it could be that, in their way of thinking, the Catholic faith, because it's so much more ritualistic—in the clothing of the minister, the decorations of the church, the statues—maybe they thought that was more religious than a Presbyterian church.

"Maybe her parents went Catholic as solace; they needed something they could see, rather than just words. Catholics have more attractive rituals compared to Presbyterians. They might have connected it with being holy; the trappings drew them."

Pastor Zingaro spoke candidly in guessing why Ida Ferguson, and, perhaps, her husband, joined the Catholic church after they so resisted Hazel's wedding at St. Mary's in Marshall.

Perhaps after Hazel's tragic death, joining the Catholic church drew them closer to her memory, or possibly they realized it is not the particular congregation that is important, but, rather, it is faith that matters most.

Or, it could have been the comfort they received in believing that they would one day be reunited with their only child—the daughter they lost so suddenly in the throes of family conflict; the daughter who dared to defy them and wed; the one who died, so tragically, with a handsome, young farmer.